The
HERITAGE BOOK
2002

The

HERITAGE
BOOK

2002

Edna McCann

HarperCollins*PublishersLtd*

THE HERITAGE BOOK 2002
Copyright © 2001 by Edna McCann.
All rights reserved. No part of this book
may be used or reproduced in any
manner whatsoever without prior written
permission except in the case of brief
quotations embodied in reviews.
For information address
HarperCollins Publishers Ltd,
55 Avenue Road, Suite 2900,
Toronto, Ontario, Canada M5R 3L2

www.harpercanada.com

HarperCollins books may be purchased
for educational, business, or sales promo-
tional use. For information please write:
Special Markets Department,
HarperCollins Canada,
55 Avenue Road, Suite 2900,
Toronto, Ontario, Canada M5R 3L2

First edition

Canadian Cataloguing in Publication Data

McCann, Edna
The Canadian heritage book

Annual.
2000
ISSN 1489-937X
ISBN 0-00-200075-X

1. Anecdotes.
2. Devotional calendars.
3. Maxims, English.
I. Title

PN6331.M32   242'.2   C99-900610-X

WEB 5 4 3 2 1

Printed and bound in Canada
Set in New Caledonia

The author gratefully acknowledges the
following sources: "Winter Sea" by Grace
R. Lloyd from *Homespun*. "I Have
Found Such Joy" from *Light of the Years*
by Grace Noll Crowell. Copyright
© 1936 Harper & Row Publishers, Inc.
Copyright © renewed 1964 by Grace
Noll Crowell. Reprinted by permission
of HarperCollins Publishers, Inc. "An
Easter Prayer" by Lelah Kinney Ayers.
"Where The Shadows Meet" by L. E.
Voswinkel. "After the Rain" by Georgia
B. Adams. "Lord Give Me Time" by
Grace E. Easley is reprinted by permis-
sion of the author. "Crab Apple Tree in
Bloom" from *Bright Harvest* by Grace
Noll Crowell. Copyright © 1952
by Grace Noll Crowell. Copyright
© renewed 1980 by Reid Crowell. Re-
printed by permission of HarperCollins
Publishers, Inc. "One Golden Gift" by
Garnett Ann Schultz is reprinted by
permission of the author. "Building A
Nation" from *My Kitchen Window* by
Edna Jaques. Copyright © 1935 Thomas
Allen & Son Limited. Reprinted by
permission of Thomas Allen & Son
Limited. "Summer is a Smile" by Molly
Elaine Johnson. "A Peck O'Maut" by
Patrick R. Chalmers. "The leaves of
autumn whisper…" by Georgia B.
Adams. "The hills of October…" by
Barton Rees Pogue.

Introduction

Each year as I prepare the stories, quotations, poems and anecdotes that make up *The Heritage Book*, I take great pleasure in recalling the experiences and people who have inspired me.

It is fitting, in a book that I hope brings comfort and joy, that I share with you the story of Charles and Mary Ann Dunscombe, two people whose courage and optimism may be a shining light of inspiration for us all.

"Chuck" was born in Detroit, Michigan, in 1928. He and Mary Ann, also a Detroit native, married at a young age and became parents of two sons, Charles Jr. and Thomas. Chuck's career as an accountant was interrupted by a stint in the army during the Korean War, but on his return he and Mary Ann shared the joys and challenges of raising their two young sons in a close-knit neighbourhood of Detroit. An avid outdoorsman, Chuck loved to fish and was teaching his children to enjoy this pastime as well. Chuck's stories of the fish they caught and "the one that got away" became legendary.

This family's idyllic life came to an abrupt end when Chuck was in a devastating car crash that left him a quadriplegic. Suddenly this tall, athletic, "always on the go" man was, at thirty years of age, destined to spend the rest of his life in a wheelchair.

For many, this would be a crushing blow from which they would never recover. Not so for Chuck or Mary Ann. With the help of family, friends and neighbours they set about making Chuck's life as fulfilled as was possible. Mary Ann, a schoolteacher, was able to continue her career as friends and neighbours came into their home daily to help with Chuck's care. Family members worked hard to make adaptations that would allow Chuck to be outdoors whenever possible. It must have been quite a sight to see him being pulled down a snowy sidewalk in his wheelchair that his father had fitted with skis!

How easy it would have been to be angry or bitter but neither Mary Ann nor Chuck chose to be so. They met the challenges of this new way of life with a sense of humour and a stong faith that life could be a joyful, rewarding experience in spite of the tremendous difficulties presented to them.

Although Chuck had only limited use of his arm and hand muscles, he was able to use a motorized wheelchair and was often seen speeding down the road on his way to visit friends.

Fate dealt Chuck another cruel blow as, in 1990, his wheelchair tipped backwards and he broke his neck again, this time slightly higher, leaving him with virtually no use of his hands. In 1995 he and Mary Ann moved to Florida as the cold weather and snow in Michigan would have left him a prisoner in his home all winter.

It was in Florida, while visiting my friend Emily,

that I met this wonderful couple. By this time Chuck's health was deteriorating as lung infections became more frequent, but he remained a cheerful and extraordinary conversationalist, knowledgeable about almost any topic you might choose. By now, Mary Ann was Chuck's sole caregiver, a job that would have been daunting for someone half her age. However, her every helpful gesture was acknowledged with a "Thank you" or perhaps a "You do that so well"—a response that she richly deserved and truly appreciated. When you were with them you could feel their tremendous love for one another.

Chuck passed away March 5, 2001. At his funeral, Chuck Jr. read a poem about the outdoors, a favourite of his father's. Son Tom eulogized his dad by paying tribute to his everlasting courage and by thanking his mother, Uncle Ian, Aunt Betty (Mary Ann's sister), Uncle Lou and the scores of other family members and friends who were able to turn a tragedy into a joy-filled life well lived.

"Rest eternal grant to him, O Lord
And let light perpetual shine on him."

I hope that you will take pleasure in the 2002 edition of *The Heritage Book* and that you will have many happy and fulfilling days in this year to come.

Edna McCann

January

Tuesday January 1

Many years ago, when I was a very young newlywed, my mother sent me a greeting card for the New Year. I have saved this card, now yellowed with age, and not a New Year's Day goes by that I don't appreciate its sound advice. I offer this poem to you today as we look forward to 365 days of a wonderful new year, 2002.

> When in your heart you wander through
> The year that's newly past,
> Tarry with its gladdest times
> And to its joy keep fast.
>
> Follow just the signs that point
> To memories of cheer;
> There's nothing gained in setting forth
> Upon the paths of fear.
>
> As you journey, stop and rest
> Where sadness does not stay.
> And should some sorrow beckon you—
> Walk another way.

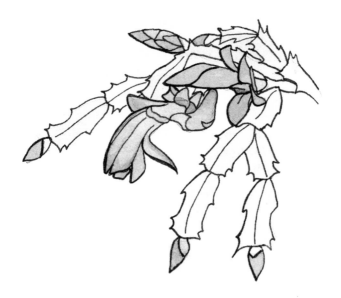

Wednesday January 2

I have always thought of myself as an optimist
and many of my friends also seem to be. I
remember my dear friend Betty, who in spite of
being bedridden for many years, was unfailingly
cheerful and a delight to be around. The closest
thing to a complaint that I ever heard Betty speak
came one afternoon near the end of her life when
she said, "Edna, I know the Lord won't send me
more trouble than I am able to bear, but there
are times when I wish He didn't have such a high
opinion of me."

To the day that she died, Betty was never
anything but optimistic. In the face of adversity,

she held fast to hope and always saw the best in everything and everyone.

It's people like Betty, never defeated by their troubles, who make it so much easier for the rest of us to contend with ours.

Thursday January 3

Don't be too concerned if the temptation to give advice is irresistible; the ability to ignore it is universal.

Friday January 4

Man does not live by words alone...despite the fact that he sometimes has to eat them.

Adlai Stevenson

Saturday January 5

My daughter Marg and I waited until today to put away our Christmas decorations. Although not an onerous task, it is time consuming. We knew we would have at least two extra hands to help us—those of my son-in-law Bruce—if we waited for a day this weekend. In hindsight, Marg and I have concluded that we might better have done it on our own.

Bruce is a chartered accountant by profession, and years at this work have made him neat and organized to a fault. As Marg and I wrapped the tree ornaments to be put away, Bruce thought it would be a good idea to label each one as we packed it in the box.

"But Bruce," said Marg very sweetly, "we put all of these ornaments on the tree every year. Why would we need to label them? We simply pull them out, unwrap them and hang them on the tree."

"Yes," said Bruce quickly, "but then you would know which ornament you were unwrapping, and while you were removing the paper, you could decide where it should go on the tree. It would make decorating much faster."

Bruce had many more ever-so-helpful hints that he was happy to share with us throughout the cleanup. Marg seemed to appreciate the advice, although I noticed after a few hours that her teeth seemed to be clenched a teeny bit as she said, "Thank you, dear," after each of Bruce's suggestions. Finally the two of us slipped off for a cup of tea and left Bruce to finish on his own. Well, at least it's over with!

Sunday January 6
Epiphany

O God, who by the leading of a star, didst manifest thy only begotten Son to the Gentiles: Mercifully grant, that we, which know thee now by faith, may after this life have the fruition of thy glorious Godhead; through Jesus Christ our Lord. Amen.

The Book of Common Prayer

Monday January 7

The strongest shield against loneliness is creative action; the heaviest armor against discouragement is joyful generosity; the greatest bulwark against despair is unselfish service.

William Arthur Ward

Tuesday January 8

Take life as it comes. If you want to give God a good laugh, tell him your plans.

Yiddish proverb

Wednesday January 9

After many wonderful, high-in-calorie holiday meals, I am usually ready for lighter fare. On a cold January evening, I enjoy a bowl of soup with biscuits and a small salad. Cauliflower soup is one of my favourites.

　　1 medium cauliflower
　　1 stalk of celery, washed and cut into 1-inch
　　　　pieces

1 thick slice lemon
2 tbsp. butter
1 medium-sized onion, peeled and diced
2 tbsp. flour
1 cup of water in which the cauliflower was cooked
3 cups chicken stock (you may substitute chicken broth)
2 tsp. salt
1/4 tsp. pepper
1 cup light cream

Cook the cauliflower, celery and slice of lemon in boiling water. When tender, drain and reserve the celery pieces and 1 cup of the water. Discard the lemon. Break the cauliflower into florets and reserve 1/2 cup of the smallest pieces for garnish. Melt the butter in a large pot and, when foaming, add the onion. Stir and cook until the onion is transparent. Add the flour. Cook and stir until well blended. Slowly add the cup of cauliflower water, celery pieces and cauliflower florets, stirring constantly, until well blended. Add stock or broth, salt and pepper. Pour this mixture into a blender and blend until the mixture is smooth. Return soup to the pot and simmer 10 to 15 minutes. Add the light cream, stir and bring just to a boil. Just before serving, add the 1/2 cup of reserved florets. Serve immediately. This recipe serves 4 as a meal or 6 as an appetizer.

Thursday January 10

Our church bulletin printed these "Ten Rules Kids Won't Learn in School." I'm not sure of the source of these lines but the message is a good one.

1. Life isn't fair, get used to it.
2. The real world won't care as much about your self-esteem as your school does. Don't let this come as a shock to you.
3. If you think your teacher is tough and has high expectations, wait until you have a boss.
4. You will not make $50,000 a year right out of high school, nor will you be a vice-president with a car phone, until you earn both.
5. Pushing a broom is not beneath your dignity. Your grandparents had a word for broom-pushing. It was "opportunity."
6. It's not your parents' fault if you mess up, so don't whine about your mistakes, learn from them.
7. Before you were born, your parents weren't as boring as they are now. They got that way from paying your bills or listening to you talk about how "cool" you are.
8. Smoking does not make you "cool."
9. Life is not divided into semesters. You don't get summers off and very few employers are interested in helping you "find yourself." Do that on your own time.

10. Some schools have abolished failing grades. Standards are set so low that almost anyone can meet them. This does not happen in real life.

Friday January 11

Time is a sort of river of passing events, and strong is its current; no sooner is a thing brought to sight than it is swept by and another takes its place, and this, too, will be swept away.

Marcus Aurelius Antonius

Saturday January 12

A good marriage is one in which each appoints the other guardian of his solitude. Once the realization is accepted that even between the closest human beings, infinite distance continues to exist, a wonderful living side by side can grow up, if they succeed in loving the distance between them which makes it possible for each to see the other whole and against a wide sky.

Rainer Maria Rilke

Sunday January 13

So teach us to number our days: that we may apply our hearts unto wisdom. Return again,

O Lord, how long? and let it repent thee concerning thy servants. O satisfy us early with thy mercy; that we may rejoice and be glad all the days of our lives.

Psalm 90:12–14

Monday January 14

My friend Marcia, a resident of Boston, Massachusetts, passed along these lovely lines for today. Anyone who has ever been by the sea in the winter will truly appreciate this poem.

Winter Sea

I love the sea, its mystery,
And surging tides have talked to me.
The rush and roar of surf tossed high
Till blue of water meets blue of sky,
But I can not leave my inland dwelling
To watch the tides receding, swelling;
So old King Winter brings to me
His imitation of the sea.
By my north door he likes to blow
A miniature wave of purest snow;
A downy crest of no mean height
He whirls on the south for my delight.
The meadow broad where we cut sweet hay
Is now a still, white, frozen bay.
Wind roars like surf on my icy strand,

Sleet strikes the panes and sounds like sand,
And winter holds for me a charm
On my snow-blocked New England farm.
Grace R. Lloyd

Tuesday January 15

Today is the birth date of Dr. Martin Luther King, Nobel Peace Prize winner and beloved African-American statesman. The following words are a fine example of the late Dr. King's credo:

"The ultimate measure of a man is not where he stands in moments of comfort and convenience, but where he stands at times of challenge and controversy."

Wednesday January 16

The truth of the matter is that you always know the right thing to do. The hard part is doing it.
General Norman Schwarzkopf

Thursday January 17

Grandparents and grandchildren do not have to do anything to make each other happy. Their happiness comes from being together.
Arthur Kornhaber

How I love to have my grandchildren come to visit. Many times we will simply sit and talk in my small kitchen while enjoying tea and cookies. On other occasions, we may play Scrabble or cards, but no matter how much or how little we do, I feel a great sense of joy in their company. I hope that they feel as I do.

Friday January 18

People are afraid of the future, of the unknown. If a man faces up to it, and takes the dare of the future, he can have some control over his destiny. That's an exciting idea to me— better than waiting with everybody else to see what's going to happen.

John H. Glenn, Jr.

Saturday January 19

My good friend Marion is a worrier. Although she knows that research has proven that worrying is bad for your health and happiness, she finds it very difficult to eliminate worries from her mind.

It's interesting to know that women worry more than they would like to, and that they worry more than men do. The probable reason for this is that women are more likely to be the ones who care for and nurture everyone. However, it is also a fact that 95 per cent of the things we worry about never happen or are beyond our ability to change.

Some good friends and I discussed the ways in which we try to eliminate, or at least control, the worry in our lives. Here are a few of the methods that have helped us.

My friend Jake discovered that taking a brisk walk helps him. Even a few minutes of aerobic exercise boosts the rate of production of serotonin, the mood-boosting brain chemical.

Muriel finds it helpful to write down the things that worry her. Since we write more slowly than we think, we slow down the thought process that churns the worry in our mind. Muriel also finds that she sees her worries much more objectively when they are written down.

I find that talking about my worries with someone else seems to reduce my concerns, even if the people I talk to don't help me solve my problems.

It is just as useless to worry as it is to tell others not to.

Sunday January 20

Lighten our darkness, Lord, we pray; and in your mercy defend us from all perils and dangers of this night; for the love of your only Son, our Saviour Jesus Christ. Amen.

An Evening Collect from
The Gelasean Sacramentary

Monday January 21

When the temperature hovers well below freezing, and the wind howls to produce a major chill factor, I have to laugh at my brother Ben's way of keeping warm. Last evening, when I spoke with him, he was sitting in front of a blazing log fire reading a seed catalogue that had arrived in the mail. Leafing through a seed book with its pictures of magnificent blossoms or succulent vegetables may seem to be a strange thing to do in January, but for Ben it is a ritual that helps him to remember the promise of spring.

"You know, Edna, when I look at these catalogues, it brings the spring and summer so vividly to my mind that I can almost feel the warmth of the sun on my back as my mind works in our gardens. Other folk may enjoy reading the works of great authors, but for me, the seed catalogues are the finest reading that I ever do."

As I feel the chill of the evening, I wonder if I, too, should be reading the garden catalogues!

Tuesday January 22

My son-in-law Bruce feels that the weather-man's reports would be more accurate if he would only stick his head out the window.

Wednesday January 23

When you have closed your doors and dark-ened your room, remember never to say that you are alone, for you are not alone; God is within, and your genius is within—and what need have they of light to see what you are doing?

Epictetus

Thursday January 24

My son-in-law John, a minister, found that lately much of his time was being given to counselling sessions with people seeking to find peace of mind. John decided to see if he could come up with a plan that would give these parish-ioners the help they felt they needed, while cutting back on the amount of this time needed to deal with their problems.

John arranged to see a group of 10 people at the same time. When they had all arrived, he said that he had to leave for an emergency and would return in about an hour. He suggested that while he was gone, they talk with each other.

When he came back, no one was in his office,

but there was a note on his desk. It read, in part, "We have heard each other's stories and decided that our own problems aren't so bad after all. Thanks John."

Friday January 25

Today is "Robbie Burns Day"—a day to celebrate for those of us who claim Scottish ancestry. My mother was very proud of her Scottish heritage and, in our home, much was made of this special day.

On my grandfather's stone in Scotland is a quote from Robert Burns.

If there is another world, he lives in bliss.
If there is none, he made the best of this.

Saturday January 26

Catharine Parr Traill was a great Canadian pioneer who settled in the vicinity of Peterborough, Ontario. The following is part of a letter written in 1834 to her relatives in England.

"You say you fear the rigours of the Canadian winters will kill me. I never enjoyed better health, nor been so good, as since it commenced. There is a degree of spirit and vigour infused into one's blood by the purity of the air that is quite exhilarating. The very snow seems whiter and more beautiful than it does in your damp, vapoury climate."

Sunday January 27

I shall light a candle of understanding in thine heart, which shall not be put out.

Esdras 14:25, The Apocrypha

Monday January 28

My husband, George, was very interested in Canadian history. I know he would have enjoyed this story of the life of George Dawson.

George, the son of William Dawson (who is known as the "father" of McGill University), was was born in Pictou, Nova Scotia, in 1849.

At the age of 10, George was stricken by an illness which left him hunchbacked. Although he was a brilliant boy who dreamed of Western exploration, it seemed that his dream would never be fulfilled, and that he would be an invalid obliged at that time to live the life of an academic.

People had not counted on his ferocious determination. Despite his handicap, he became a geologist and natural scientist. In 1873, the North American Boundary Commission hired Dawson. It was his first job in what was to become a lifetime of exploration into the Canadian Northwest.

He made many exploratory journeys, some of epic proportions, on foot and on horseback and earned the nickname "Skookum Tumtum"—brave, cheery man—since this was how his contemporaries saw him. He was the first educated man to explore and map the Yukon Territory. Dawson City is named in his honour.

In the words of Friedrich Nietzsche:
"What does not destroy me, makes me strong."

Tuesday January 29

Shared laughter creates a bond of friendship. When people laugh together, they cease to be young and old, master and pupil, worker and driver. They have become a single group of human beings, enjoying their experience.

W. Lee Grant

Wednesday January 30

My friend Jake Frampton stopped by this evening. My former readers know that Jake owns a used book-store and often brings me books that he knows I will enjoy reading. Today was no exception. Jake brought me a number of "whodunits" as he knows that mysteries are special favourites of mine. In return for Jake's kindness, I made dinner for us to share. A life-long bachelor, he enjoys eating a meal that he has not had to prepare. Jake is a friend with whom I feel completely comfortable and it is so nice that we can give each other these special gifts—books, dinners and friendship. I feel very lucky.

Thursday January 31

All the troubles of life come upon us because we refuse to sit quietly for a while each day in our rooms.

Blaise Pascal

February

Friday February 1

The real voyage of discovery consists not in seeking new landscapes, but in having new eyes.

Marcel Proust

Saturday February 2

This is the day when we find out whether or not we will face prolonged winter weather.

Groundhogs in Wiarton, Ontario, and in Punxsutawney, Pennsylvania, become our "weather forecasters."

According to tradition, when the animals leave their holes on this date, they reportedly check to see if they can see their shadows. If they do, they will return to their underground homes and we will be in for another six weeks of winter weather.

Many people believe that these little prognosticators are very accurate and, indeed, studies over the past few years seem to bear this out.

I, for one, am hoping that the winter will have an early end!

Sunday February 3

Praise the Lord, O my soul; I will praise the Lord as long as I live; I will sing praises unto my God as long as I have being.

Psalm 146:1–2

Monday February 4

Reading books in one's youth is like looking at the moon through a crevice; reading books in middle age is like looking at the moon in one's courtyard; and reading books in old age is like looking at the moon on an open terrace. This is because the depth of your benefit from reading varies in proportion to the depth of your own experience.

Chang Ch'ao

Tuesday February 5

My brother Ben has been feeling under the weather for a few weeks now. He was able to see his family physician earlier today and I laughed when Ben told me of their conversation. After Ben listed his symptoms, the doctor said, "You know Ben, I'm a doctor, not a magician. Many of these ailments come with old age and I can't make you young again."

"I don't want to be young again, Doctor," Ben replied. "I just want to know that I am going to go on getting older."

Wednesday February 6

Although I find the cold of winter difficult to endure, I do love the beauty of a snowy day. I thank the unknown author for these lines for today.

Beautiful, Beautiful Snow

A winter world's a soft white world
Of drifts and glistening flakes
And boughs and overhangings high
And sculptured pristine lakes.

And often in this magnitude
Of soft white winter driven snow
Are footprints small, belonging to
Some creature on the go,
Who stood and smelled the clear crisp air
Then tracked upon his way
Excited by the wonderworld
That held the land in sway.

O winter world, O soft white world,
In you I see God's touch,
And feel that He created you
For those He loved so much.

A promise too, is there ahead,
For when the snow has gone
He'll leave His springtime world for us
To love and look upon.

Thursday February 7

Marg and I recently attended a baby shower for a young neighbour who is expecting her first child. Tracy asked that we mothers include with our gifts a piece of advice on something that we would have done differently in raising our children. She heard some very interesting suggestions and I offer several of these for you today.

"The most difficult decision that I had to make was whether I would go back to my job or stay home and raise my children. I thought I really needed to be a career woman, but when I missed my son's first steps, along with many of his other milestones, I knew that I had to be at home. My advice? If you can possibly afford to stay home with your children, do it."

Mary

"Give your children responsibilities at an early age. If you do everything for them they will expect it long after they are able to do things on their own."

Julie

"I would spend more time building sand castles or blowing bubbles with my children and less time worrying about how neat my house was."

Glenna

"I would keep a journal of daily life when my children were young. You think you'll remember everything, but you don't."

Marcia

Friday February 8
Andy Rooney once made this wise observation:

"There are two kinds of savers. The first is the practical saver who keeps strings, bags and old aluminum foil as a practical matter. And then there's the sentimental saver. The sentimental saver can't stand the idea of throwing out any memory of his life."

Saturday February 9
Success lies not in achieving what you aim at, but in aiming at what you ought to achieve, and pressing forward, sure of achievement here, or if not here, hereafter.

R. F. Horton

Sunday February 10
I will give thanks to the Lord with my whole heart; I will tell of all thy wonderful deeds. I will be glad and exalt in Thee; I will sing praise to thy name, O Most High.

Psalm 9:1–2

WINTER PEACE

Monday February 11

I have not much patience with a thing of beauty that must be explained to be understood. If it does need added interpretation by someone other than the creator, then I question its purpose.

Charlie Chaplin

These words came to mind this past weekend when I attended an art auction with my daughter Julia. Julia is able to appreciate art in many forms while my taste is much more plebeian. The more a painting resembles a photograph, the better I like it. Before the auction, Julia and I spent almost an hour viewing the various works, and it was extremely difficult for me to suppress a chuckle or two as I tried to understand a few of the more "modern" works. One image, titled *Running Stallion*, strongly resembled a place mat on which I had spilled hot chocolate. I saw nothing that bore the least likeness to a horse.

Fortunately for the artist, someone with taste in art that was very different from mine chose to pay more than $1,500 for the work. My, how I wish I hadn't cleaned my hot chocolate spill. Who knows how much my "work" might have fetched?

Tuesday February 12

Most quarrels, like muddy water, will clear if you don't keep stirring them up.

Wednesday February 13

Ash Wednesday

Today is Ash Wednesday, the first day of Lent. A dear friend who passed away several years ago, Canon Roland Hill, said that Lent should be a positive time. Although many choose to give up something in their lives at this time, Canon Hill suggested that you should plan to add something worthwhile as well.

In our family, we have chosen to adopt a child in South America. For a modest sum each month this child will receive good food, clean water to drink and school supplies. This, for us, is the message of giving at Easter.

Thursday February 14

Valentine's Day

I do not need a fancy heart
With Cupid's dart and bow,
To tell me in a flowery verse
What I already know.
I do not need a costly gift

Presented as a sign,
That though the years have come and gone
I'm still your Valentine.

I only need your loving smile
Each time I look your way....
For this to be from start to end
A perfect Valentine's Day.

Author unknown

Friday February 15

Those born with a talent which is meant to be used find their greatest joy in using it.

Johann Wolfgang von Goethe

Saturday February 16

In this day and age when we are bombarded by advertisements on television, in newspapers and on the Internet, it is important to teach children to be knowledgeable consumers. How do we teach children to resist commercial hype or to question those "too-good-to-be-true" messages directed at them on a daily basis?

Experts offer many suggestions to parents to help their children become discriminating buyers. Here are a few that I think are applicable not just for children, but for all of us.

1. Get the facts before buying. Don't take anything for granted about an advertised product, especially high-tech items. Product-rating guides will give you all the information you need before making your purchase.
2. Try before you buy. Ask those who are selling the product whether you can test, or even rent, a demonstration unit before you buy it.
3. Know exactly what you are buying. Are there any additional costs, such as shipping charges, charges for assembly, setup or delivery? Is other equipment necessary to make the product usable?
4. Don't let fancy packaging fool you. Many brand-name products are available under different names at a much lower cost.

Sunday February 17

Almighty God, bestow upon us the meaning of words, the light of understanding, the nobility of diction, and the faith of thy true nature. And grant that what we believe, we may also speak.

St. Hilary

Monday February 18

I have touched on this topic before, but I feel so strongly about it that I am commenting again on organ donation.

Making the decision to donate an organ can turn a tragic loss of a life into a lifesaving act for countless others. Did you know that people die every day waiting for an organ transplant? One donor can save up to eight lives with the donation of his or her internal organs. As well, one person's skin tissue could help as many as 50 burn victims; bone marrow may assist cancer sufferers and corneas may restore sight.

Knowing that an organ donation is literally a "gift of life," should we not consider our donation a natural part of the process of dying?

Here in Canada, we rank low on the list of countries whose organ donations exceed a certain number. Why is that? Are we really so selfish?

Please, won't you and your family consider this magnificent act of giving?

"Don't take your organs with you. Heaven knows we need them here."

Tuesday February 19

Marg, Bruce and I have spent many hours this past week glued to the television. We've been watching our wonderful Canadian athletes compete at the Olympic Winter Games in Salt Lake City, Utah. I never cease to marvel at the incredible level of skill that the young men and women display at this spectacular competition. I had a bit of fun coming up with some questions about the winter Olympics and thought you might like to try my little quiz.

Questions

1. In what year was ice hockey introduced as an Olympic event?
2. Were the Olympics ever cancelled, and if so, why?
3. What was the last year in which the summer and winter games were held in the same year?
4. What was unusual about the Olympic games held in Paris in 1900?
5. When did the Olympic flame first burn from the opening to the closing of the games?

Answers

1. 1920, at the games of Antwerp, Belgium.
2. Yes, in 1940 and 1944 because of World War II.
3. 1992
4. There were more athletes than spectators.
5. In 1928, in Amsterdam, The Netherlands.

Wednesday February 20

Yesterday is but today's memory and tomorrow is today's dream. And let today embrace the past with remembrance and the future with longing.

Kahlil Gibran

One of the most wonderful gifts with which we are blessed is the ability to recreate delightful experiences of the past. Very often, on a cold winter's day when I am trapped indoors, I enjoy taking the time to recall many pleasant times that I have spent with my family and friends. It is during these reflections that I realize how much I have to look forward to in the days to come.

Thursday February 21

Sometimes I wonder
What would they think if they could know
All the changes, all the pressures;
Would they fume and fuss
The way we often do?
Would they fight against the tide?
Or, would they,
Because they share things veiled to us,
Accept God's Master Plan, and wait?

George McCann

Friday February 22

Winter has a very special beauty, its own particular joys. Snow-covered hills are alive with sleds and the sounds of children's laughter. Skiers and snowboarders seem to have wings as they fly down the slopes. Every frozen pond is a figure skater's paradise or a hockey player's Mecca.

Saturday February 23

If one sets aside time for a business appointment or a shopping expedition, that is accepted as inviolable. But if one says, "I cannot come because that is my hour to be alone," one is considered rude, egotistical or strange. What a commentary on our civilization.

Anne Morrow Lindbergh

Sunday February 24

Teach me, good Lord, to serve thee as thou deservest, to give and not count the cost—to fight and not heed the wounds—to toil and not seek to rest—to labour and not ask for reward, save that of knowing that we do Thy will through Jesus Christ our Lord.

St. Ignatius Loyola

Monday February 25

Most of us have seen brief conflicts between parents and children. How I have admired the skillful way that some parents react, and realized how unfortunate are the ways other parents handle such incidents.

Many people equate punishment with discipline. In fact, punishment is only a very small part of discipline. Children need guidance and they must know what is expected of them. Discipline must be consistent; if we expect them to be polite and have good manners at home, children need to understand that these same standards apply wherever they are.

All children test their parents to find the limit of their tolerance. Lucky the girl or boy who has these limits clearly established.

Tuesday February 26

One of my fondest childhood memories is of winter days spent playing in the attic of my parents' home.

Our attic was filled with "treasures" that could transform three young children into princesses, pirates or any other figment of the imagination.

In those days, nearly all homes were built with attics, and families saved trunks of old clothes, toys and any number of interesting articles that weren't being used but were too good to throw away. We children would spend hours amusing ourselves with plays or parades using this stored bounty.

I think children today miss out on a wonderful way to use their imagination.

Wednesday February 27

Samuel Johnson said, "Hope is itself a species of happiness, and, perhaps, the chief happiness which the world affords." Many others have spoken of hope and I offer just a few of their thoughts for you today.

Everything that is done in the world is done by hope.

Martin Luther King, Jr.

Hope is the thing with feathers
That perches in the soul—
And sings the tunes without the words
And never stops at all.

Emily Dickinson

Hope is wishing for a thing to come true; faith is believing that it will come true.

Norman Vincent Peale

Hope is like the sun, which, as we journey toward it, casts the shadows of our burden behind us.

Samuel Smiles

Thursday February 28

Comedian Jack Benny and his wife, Mary Livingston Benny, unlike many couples in Hollywood whose marriages are short-lived, were happily wed for 48 years. There is a wonderful story that actually shows the depth of Jack's love for Mary.

The day after his death in 1974, a single long-stemmed rose was delivered to Mary. Day after day, week after week, the flowers continued to arrive. Mary called the florist to find out who was sending the roses, her favourite flower.

The florist explained that quite some time before Jack had passed away, he had stopped in to order a bouquet for his wife. As he was leaving he turned back and said, "If anything should happen to me, I want you to send a single rose to Mary every day."

Jack had, in fact, made a provision in his will that would ensure one red rose be delivered to Mary every day for the rest of her life.

March

The Weaver

My life is but a weaving
Between my Lord and me....
I may not choose the colours;
He knows what they should be;
For He can view the pattern
Upon the upper side,
Whilst I can see it only
On this, the underside.

Sometimes He weaveth sorrow,
Which seemeth strange to me;
But I will trust His judgment
And work on faithfully.
'Tis He who fills the shuttle;
He knows just what is best;
So I shall weave in earnest
And leave Him with the rest.

Not till the loom is silent
And the shuttles cease to fly,
Shall God unroll the canvas,
And explain the reason why

The dark threads are as needful,
In the weaver's skillful hand,
As the threads of gold and silver
In the pattern He has planned.

Author unknown

Saturday March 2

I have been so fortunate throughout my life to have many close friends. My dearest friend was my husband, George, whose early passing left an enormous void in my life. Although no one could ever replace him, the love and support of my family and friends have made my life a wonderfully happy one. I offer for you today others' ideas of friendship.

The ornaments of our house are the friends that frequent it.

Ralph Waldo Emerson

A friend is a person with whom you dare to be yourself.

Frank Crane

Friendships begun in this world can be taken up again in heaven, never to be broken off.

St. Francis de Sales

Heaven gives us friends to bless the present scene.

Edward Young

A constant friend is a thing rare and hard to find.

Plutarch

A faithful friend is a strong defense; and he that hath found such an one, hath found a treasure.

Apocrypha

The things our friends do with us and for us form a portion of our lives; they strengthen our personality.

Goethe

Sunday March 3

> All people that on earth do dwell
> Sing to the Lord with cheerful voice
> Him serve with mirth, His praise forth tell
> Come ye before Him and rejoice.

Scottish Psalter (1650) Based on Psalm 100

Monday March 4

My son-in-law John, a minister, was recently asked to be a substitute speaker at a large interdenominational gathering in Montreal. He was replacing a well-known preacher and could have found this request very intimidating. Fortunately he remembered this story and, in the telling of it, managed to bring the group together in a common bond of laughter.

"Before Harry Emerson Fosdick had become the renowned pastor of New York's Riverdale Church, he was asked to substitute for a well-known minister who was seriously ill.

The gentleman making the introductions rambled on in superlatives about the speaker who should have been there. Finally he said, 'We are fortunate to have young Harry Fosdick in his place.'

A smiling Fosdick acknowledged the introduction. 'I'm reminded,' he said, 'of the time I was travelling through a small town and saw a banner strung across the main street that said ANNUAL STRAWBERRY FESTIVAL.

Under this banner was another, smaller banner that said, 'Due to the drought, prunes will be served.'"

Tuesday March 5

I believe that the best way to prepare for a future life is to be kind, live one day at a time, and do the work you can do the best, doing it as well as you can.

Elbert Hubbard

Wednesday March 6

In November 2000, Texas Governor George W. Bush and Vice President Al Gore were locked in a battle to become the president of the United States of America. It was a particularly tight race and Democrats and Republicans stood solidly behind their candidates. One gentleman, James E. Fete, Sr., of Canton, Ohio, was a staunch supporter of Governor Bush. When he passed away before the election, his adult sons and daughter wanted to give their father the last word—and they did.

In the obituary for their father, they listed his many accomplishments, including service in the Korean War and 39 years with Ohio Bell Telephone. It was the last line that was unusual. "In lieu of flowers, Vote Bush!"

As we know, it took many weeks of counting and recounting and an unprecedented United States Supreme Court decision, but Governor George W. Bush did, in fact, become the President of the United States.

Thursday March 7

Thanks to our friend Will, Marg and I have some beautiful spring flowers in many corners of our home. Will, gardener extraordinaire, taught us how to force bulbs, a method whereby spring flower bulbs are fooled into flowering early. It really is quite simple and the results are spectacular!

You will need to spend a bit of time searching nurseries, florist shops or catalogues for bulbs labelled "pre-chilled" or "ready for forcing." These bulbs have been stored, usually for about 12 weeks, at approximately 3°C. These bulbs should be planted, pointed side up, in pots that have a drainage hole, a layer of gravel (for drainage) and ordinary potting soil. Crocuses and daffodils need to be planted about an inch deep. Tulips and hyacinths need their points above soil level, while amaryllis and paperwhites may also be planted in pebbles or even in a narrow-topped vase to be grown in water alone.

The potted bulbs should be kept in a cool, dark place and watered about once a week until pale shoots start to appear. When these shoots grow to a few inches, the pot should be moved to a warm, bright location. Turning the pots will ensure that the stems grow straight. Most of the flowers should bloom in two to three weeks.

Unusual pots, vases, baskets or urns may be used to make a wonderful display that will brighten any room.

Friday March 8

I have never met a person whose greatest need was anything other than real, unconditional love. You can find it in a simple act of kindness towards someone who needs help. There is no mistaking love. You feel it in your heart. It is a common fibre of life, the flame that heats our soul, supplies passion to our lives and energizes our spirit. It is our connection to God and to each other.

Elisabeth Kubler-Ross, M.D.

Saturday March 9

Nostalgia is the halfway house by which you love the past and the sweet things in it without actually committing yourself to the nonsense that life was better then.

Henry Mitchel

Sunday March 10

They that wait upon the Lord shall renew their strength; they shall mount up with wings as eagles; they shall run, and not be weary, and they shall walk and not faint.

Isaiah 40:31

Monday March 11

The poetic works of Grace Noll Crowell have always appealed to me. This next poem is one of my favourites; I hope you will enjoy it as well.

I Have Found Such Joy

I have found such joy in simple things:
A plain clean room, a nut brown loaf of
    bread,
A cup of milk, a kettle as it sings,
A shelter of a roof above my head,
And in a leaf-laced square upon the floor,
Where yellow sunlight glimmers through a
    door.

I have found such joy in things that fill
My quiet days: a curtain's blowing grace,
A growing plant upon my window sill,
A rose fresh-cut and placed with a vase,
A table cleared, a lamp beside a chair,
And books I long have loved beside me there.

Oh, I have found such joy! I wish I might
Tell everyone who goes seeking far
For some illusive feverish delight,
That very close to home the greatest joys are:
These elemental things, old as are the race,
Yet never through the ages commonplace.

Tuesday March 12

The pathway to success is serving humanity. By no other means is it possible, and this truth is so plain and patent that even very simple folk recognize it.

Elbert Hubbard

Wednesday March 13

Nature is man's teacher. She unfolds her treasures to his search, unseals his eye, illumes his mind and purifies his heart; an influence breathes from all the sights and sounds of her existence.

Alfred Billings Street

Thursday March 14

At this time of year, when many families choose to travel to warmer climes, the highways and airports become very busy places. Often at these peak travel times, when delays are nearly inevitable, it is not uncommon for tempers to fray. My friend Emily related her experience at an airport in the southern United States.

"Edna, I was in a lineup to check in for my flight to Philadelphia. Because of poor weather in the North, there had been numerous delays or cancellations. The lines of travellers checking in stretched halfway across the terminal and many of us were hungry, tired and frustrated by the long wait.

One man, well dressed, carrying a briefcase, and obviously agitated, marched past all of us who were in line, went right to the counter, slapped his ticket down and said to the airline clerk, 'I have to get on this flight and I HAVE to have a first-class ticket!'

'I'll do what I can sir, but I need to take care of these people in line first.'

'Do you know who I am?' the irate man shouted at the clerk.

Calmly the clerk picked up his microphone and said, 'Good afternoon, ladies and gentlemen. We have a problem here at check-in gate 14. There is a gentleman here who doesn't know who he is. If any one of you could help, please let us know.'

There was some good-natured laughing and applause, and the man was last seen slinking to the rear of the line."

SPRING CLEANING

Friday March 15

If watching TV has taught me anything, it's that there are an infinite number of once-in-a-lifetime opportunities.

Richard C. Miller

Saturday March 16

Tomorrow is St. Patrick's Day, a day for the "wearin' o' the green" for all who can claim Irish heritage.

Ireland's patron saint was born on the west coast of England or Scotland—the accounts of the place and date vary widely. Captured by Irish pirates at age 16, he was kept as a slave for six years. While tending his master's herd, he spent many hours praying. In his autobiography he wrote, "I said as many as a hundred prayers.... I used to stay in the woods and on the mountain, and before the dawn, I would be aroused to prayer, in snow and frost and rain...because then the spirit was fervent within."

After he escaped, he found his family and trained for the priesthood. He was sent as a missionary to Ireland by the Pope where he travelled all over the country founding churches and monasteries. Patrick was the major influence in converting Ireland to the Christian faith. His writings are the earliest British Christian literature.

To all my Irish friends, a very happy St. Patrick's Day.

Sunday March 17

Many people will remember Dag Hammarskjöld as the second Secretary General of the United Nations, but fewer people know that Hammarskjöld was a very spiritual man and that his diary, *Markings*, was published after his death in 1961. This poem comes from this book.

God the Artist

You take the pen,
and the lines dance.
You take the flute,
and the notes shimmer.
You take the brush,
And the colours sing.

So all things have meaning and beauty in that space beyond time where you are. How then, can I hold anything back from You?

Monday March 18

Good friends of mine recently celebrated their golden wedding anniversary. At the celebration, someone asked the secret of their happy marriage. We all laughed as Elaine said, "I think it helped a lot to know from the very beginning that the path of true love didn't lead over to my mother's when things got difficult."

Tuesday March 19

No matter how old a mother is, she watches her middle-aged children for signs of improvement.

F. Scott-Maxwell

Wednesday March 20

We Canadians are a very ingenious and creative group, but because we are extremely modest, many people are unaware of some of our most interesting inventions. Here are just a few of the things of which we may be justifiably—and outspokenly—proud.

In 1922–23, Dr. Frederick Banting and a medical research team at the University of Toronto isolated the hormone for insulin, thus providing a method of treatment for diabetes. Until then, diabetes was usually terminal.

Arthur Sicard of St. Leonard, Quebec, came up with something that made Canadian winters a little easier to bear. Using the rotating blades of a thresher as an idea, Sicard invented the snowblower in 1926.

In 1891, James Naismith of Almont, Ontario,

nailed two peach baskets to the balcony of a gymnasium and, with two teams using a soccer ball to "dunk" in the basket, he invented the game of basketball.

Doctors Fredrick Tisdale, Theodore Drake and Allan Brown created "Pablum," the wonderful and nutritious baby food that has been fed to babies for generations.

Norman Breaky revolutionized the paint industry in 1940 with his invention of the labour-saving paint roller.

Thursday March 21

Spring arrives today and I thank the unknown author of these thoughts that really made me feel springlike.

Because

Because I have seen the flowers,
   I know what colour is...
   What fragrance is ... what beauty is...
Because I have seen the springtime's
   divine awakening,
   I know what hope is...
   what faith is... what joy is...
Because I have seen the eagle soar
   and tall pines sway in the breeze
   I know what grace is...
Because I have listened to the birds

carol at daybreak,
I know what majesty is...
what thanksgiving is...
Because I have looked upon the mountain, the
oceans and the trees,
I know what majesty is... what grandeur is...
what poise is...
Because I have seen the sun, the moon
and stars in their ponderous courses,
I know what power is...
Contemplation of these revelations
Mounts faith almost to understanding.

Friday March 22

Along with the arrival of spring our family celebrates the birthday of my great-granddaugh-
ter Bethany. She is a child with a wonderfully
sunny disposition, so it seems appropriate that she
was born on the first day of spring.

"The best thing about spring is that it always
comes when it is most needed."

Saturday March 23

God is like a mirror. The mirror never
changes but everybody who looks in it sees
something different.

Rabbi Harold Kushner

Sunday March 24
Palm Sunday

Let not your heart be troubled; ye believe in God, believe also in me. In my father's house are many mansions; if it were not so, I would have told you. I go to prepare a place for you. And if I go and prepare a place for you, I will come again and receive you unto myself; that where I am, there ye may be also.

John 14:1–3

Monday March 25

Envy can be a positive motivator. Let it inspire you to work harder for what you want.

Robert Bringle

Tuesday March 26

A good many people do not believe in the efficiency of prayer because the Lord gives them what they deserve instead of what they ask for.

Bob Edwards

Wednesday March 27

What sunshine is to flowers, smiles are to humanity. They are but trifles, to be sure, but scattered along life's pathway, the good they do is inconceivable.

Joseph Addison

Thursday March 28

It is difficult to say what is impossible, for the dream of yesterday is the hope of today, and the reality of tomorrow.

R. H. Goddard

Friday March 29

Good Friday

For God so loved the world that He gave His only begotten Son, that whosoever believeth in Him should not perish, but have everlasting life.

John 3:16

Saturday March 30

How much I enjoy our family get-togethers for the special times. Today Marg, Mary, Julia and I spent many hours getting ready for our Easter dinner tomorrow. Julia, who is very creative, had many wonderful ideas for the four of us to work on to make our table particularly festive.

Our napkin rings are not only attractive, they

are delicious as well. Using a needle and some heavy thread, we threaded jelly beans and, after tying off each end of the thread, we tied the ends together to make a circle (a little vegetable oil on the needle made it easier). Two or three strands of jelly beans on each napkin will delight adults and children alike.

Julia also brought a white sheet to use as a table cloth. After we had set the table, she used a felt marker to draw two or three "eggs" around each place setting. She put coloured makers in a cup to be shared so that each family member could decorate his or her eggs. We hope to save the cloth to be used another year.

Our preparations will make the day special, of course, but the loveliest part of tomorrow will be our time spent rejoicing in the strength of our faith and belief in the message of Easter, the life to come after death.

Sunday March 31

An Easter Prayer
May the glorious dawn of Easter morn
And all that it imparts,
Bring hope anew to everyone
And love to troubled hearts!

May the glory of our risen Lord,
Shine so the world may find
True brotherhood, with prayer and faith,
For peace to all mankind.

May the beauty of this glad springtime
Bring a radiant joy and cheer—
And Easter's story told again,
Bring our Saviour very near.

Lelah Kinney Ayers

April

Where The Shadows Meet

Once more young April stirs our hearts—
The fields, late fallow, now are green;
From bud and root a new life starts,
And in the garden here is seen
A golden-chaliced daffodil.

In leafy glades the thrushes spill
Their song of rapturous delight;
No more the winter's icy chill
Can mar our joy with sudden blight,
For Spring, with sandals on her feet,

Steps lightly where the shadows meet
Long shadows through the purple haze.
Again the quickening pulses beat
As down the passing years we gaze,
While time on winged feet departs,
And it is April in our hearts.

L. E. Voswinkel

Tuesday April 2

It is great to have friends when one is young, but it is still more so when you are getting old. When we are young, friends are, like everything else, a matter of course. In our old days, we know what it means to have them.

Edward Grieg

Wednesday April 3

As I grow older I find that I cherish my friendships as I seldom did as a young woman. When I was young, I was busy as a clergyman's wife, and mother of three little daughters. Many of my friends were members of the parish (and also mothers of small children) who were as busy as I was. We would see each other frequently, but our families held a much more important place in all of our daily activities and they took a significant amount of time.

As our children grew up and moved out, we had more time and energy for our friendships. We became close as we were able to share more of ourselves and build intimate relationships.

Now as I live in my "golden years," many old friends have passed away. I recognize that some small part of me dies with these friends' passing and that the time I have to spend with those who remain may be limited. For this reason, I try to keep in close touch with these wonderful people who so enrich my life.

"A friend is what the heart needs all the time."

Henry Van Dyke

Thursday April 4

As an avid reader and book lover, I appreciate James Freeman Clarke's comments on books.

"When I consider what some books have done for the world, and what they are doing, how they keep up our hope, awaken new courage and faith, soothe pain, give an ideal life to those whose hours

are cold and hard, bind together distant ages and foreign lands, create new worlds of beauty, bring down truth from heaven; I give eternal blessings for this gift, and thank God for books."

Friday April 5

Unlike some authors, American writer Robert Benchley had the ability to make fun of himself. He once remarked:

"It took me fifteen years to discover that I had no talent for writing, but I couldn't give up because by that time I was too famous."

Saturday April 6

Happiness is the only good. The place to be happy is here. The time to be happy is now. The way to be happy is to help make others so.

Robert G. Ingersoll

Sunday April 7

Some years ago, during Canada's centennial year, the Canadian Interfaith Conference published an anthology of 185 prayers to be recited in houses of worship all across the country. One of the simplest and most beautiful litanies in the prayer booklet was an ancient

Blackfoot prayer. Please enjoy these beautiful words with me today.

> O Great Spirit, Creator of all things;
> Human beings, trees, grass, berries.
> Help us, be kind to us.
> Let us be happy on earth.
> Let us lead our children
> To a good life and old age.
> These our people; give them good minds
> To love one another.
>
> O Great Spirit,
> Be kind to us.
> Give these people the favour
> To see green trees,
> Green grass, flowers and berries
> This next spring;
> So we all meet again
> O Great Sprit
> We ask of you.

Monday April 8

We are always complaining that our days are few, and acting as though there would be no end to them.

Tuesday April 9

Marg and I try to spend two mornings a week helping out at our local elementary school. Any of you who are, or ever have been, teachers, know just what a difficult and demanding job it is.

What does a teacher need to be successful? My granddaughter Phyllis, a former teacher, gave me this list.

A teacher needs
The education of a college president,
The executive ability of a financier,
The humility of a deacon,
The adaptability of a chameleon,
The hope of an optimist,
The courage of a hero,
The wisdom of a serpent,
The gentleness of a dove,
The patience of Job,
The grace of God, and
The persistence of the devil.

Wednesday April 10

Arbor Day was first celebrated April 10, 1872, in the state of Nebraska.

Oliver Wendell Holmes once said:

"When we plant a tree, we are doing what we can to make our planet a more wholesome and happier dwelling place for those who come after us, if not for ourselves."

Thursday April 11

Ours is a family of chocolate lovers! No special occasion is complete for us unless there has been something yummy made from chocolate. This next recipe is one of our particular favourites.

Chocolate Delight

3 tbsp. plus 1/4 cup sugar
6 tbsp. butter or margarine
4 ounces semisweet chocolate
1/4 cup heavy or whipping cream
1/4 cup all-purpose flour
1/2 tsp. vanilla extract
2 large eggs
2 large egg yolks
chocolate shavings (for garnish)

1. Preheat oven to 400°F. Grease eight 6-ounce ramekins or custard cups; sprinkle with 3 tablespoons sugar.
2. In a 3-quart saucepan, heat margarine or butter with chocolate and cream over low heat until melted and smooth, stirring occasionally. Remove saucepan from heat, whisk in flour and vanilla until blended.

3. In medium bowl, with mixer at high speed, beat eggs, egg yolks, and remaining 1/4 cup sugar until very thick and pale yellow—about 10 minutes. With a rubber spatula, gently fold egg mixture into chocolate mixture, one-third at a time, until blended.

4. Pour batter into ramekins, filling each about three-quarters full. Place ramekins in a 15-inch x 10 1/2-inch jelly roll pan for easier handling. Bake 9 to 10 minutes until the edge of the cake is set but the centre is slightly jiggly.

5. Cool in pan on wire rack for 5 minutes. Run a small knife around the sides of the ramekins. Invert onto dessert plates, sprinkle with shaved chocolate and serve immediately. Serves 8.

Friday April 12

How is it that our memory is good enough to retain the least triviality that happens to us, and yet not good enough to recollect how often we have told it to the same person.

Duc de la Rochefoucauld

Saturday April 13

Spring is a time when I greatly miss my old home on the east coast. There was something about air in the spring that brought out a bright new spirit in all of us. The sight of the boats setting off again to fish and the smell of the new catches remains fixed in my mind to this day. Sometimes when I am out walking, I fancy that I can hear the sound of gulls in the wind-song of the trees.

"God gave us memories that we might have roses in December," or for me, that I might be reminded of a fishing village in April.

Sunday April 14

> Our Lord took death upon Himself
> On that cruel cross of pain,
> And those who look in faith to Him
> Eternal life shall gain!

Johnson

Monday April 15

Until we have faced some great adversity in this life, it is hard to know how we will react. I like to think that I would be able to handle misfortune with courage but until put to the test, it is difficult to know.

I greatly admire the bravery of people who, through some misfortune, are forced to deal with difficult times.

One person of outstanding courage who comes to mind is the leading man in many films, American actor Christopher Reeve. Probably best known for his role as Superman, he was also an expert horseman. On May 27, 1995, while competing in a three-day equestrian event in Culpeper County, Virginia, he fell on his head as his horse was completing a jump. That fall would change his life forever. He awoke in the hospital a quadriplegic—his neck broken between the first and second vertebrae—and unable to breathe without a respirator. At one point while in hospital he said to his wife, "Perhaps we should let me go." His wife would have none of that kind of talk and between them they decided that Christopher's high profile could be of help in focusing government funding on research for spinal cord injuries.

Christopher firmly believes that he will walk again, and to that end he endures hours of physiotherapy each day. As well, he works tirelessly to raise funds for others who have also suffered a spinal-cord injury. He truly is a man of courage.

Tuesday April 16

"Remember that you ought to behave in life as you would at a banquet. As something is being passed around, it comes to you; stretch out your hand and take a portion of it politely. It passes on; do not detain it. Or, it has not yet come to you; do not project your desire to meet it, but wait until it comes in front of you."

This interesting analogy was written by Epictetus, born in the year 60 A.D. It's hard to imagine that advice written nearly 2,000 years ago is still pertinent today.

Wednesday April 17

How beautiful the world appears
After the rain
As sunbeams softly play upon
The earth again.

I lift my eyes in time to see
The rainbow fade;
The tears of nature stand up tall
On leaf and blade.

They glisten in the sunglow
Like crystals rare;
They linger like an evening hymn,
Or a morning prayer.

The clouds roll back like ancient scrolls
After the rain,
And there in grand pursuit, I see
The sun again.

Thanks to Georgia B. Adams
for her beautiful work, "After the Rain."

Thursday April 18

Learn from the mistakes of others; you can't possibly live long enough to make them all yourself.

Friday April 19

Reputation is what men and women think of us; character is what God and angels know of us.

Thomas Paine

Saturday April 20

At this time of year, many schools are planning special trips for the older students. Often these excursions are several days long and involve being away from home and family.

Some years ago, my great-grandson Geoffrey spent a week away with a group of youngsters from his school. The group was being trained in outdoor survival, and during his time away, Geoff sent home this postcard.

"Dear Mom and Dad,

There are 94 students on this trip. I wish there were 93!

Love, Geoffrey."

Sunday April 21

To every thing there is a season, and a time to every purpose under heaven.

Ecclesiastes 3:1

Monday April 22

It has often been said that experience is the greatest teacher. A child may read about the ocean, but until he has seen its vastness, the majesty of its waves, or felt the salt water on his skin, he really cannot understand the ocean.

Many writers have expressed their thoughts on experience and today I offer just a few of their ideas.

We learn from experience. A man never wakes up his second baby just to see it smile.

Grace Williams

Experience is not what happens to a man. It is what a man does with what happens to him.

Aldous Huxley

Experience is what makes you recognize a mistake when you make it again.

F. P. Jones

Life is a series of experiences, each one of which

SPRING FLOWERS

makes us bigger, even though it is sometimes hard to realize this.

Henry Ford

Experience is the only teacher that gives the test first and the lesson later.

Tuesday April 23

This past weekend, Marg, Bruce and I got involved in that yearly ritual, spring cleaning. I'm not sure how it happens, but it appears that each winter we seem to accumulate more items that need to be packed away and less space in which to store them. This means that we need to be more creative when it comes to finding storage areas. Fortunately, Marg reads women's magazines and found some excellent suggestions.

Bruce made a window seat under the bay window in the living room that has a lift-up lid and space for a number of larger items.

Marg found some good-sized boxes in which we can store our winter clothing. These boxes will slide neatly under our beds and allow us to use our closets for summer wear only.

The space between our kitchen cabinets and the ceiling provides a wonderful place for large bowls and platters that are seldom used. Marg found some lovely wicker baskets and we packed these large dishes inside. The baskets look very attractive and have freed up a number of kitchen cupboards for our use.

I have found a rather sneaky place to stash some things—under the skirted table beside my bed.

Perhaps you may find other more creative ways to store your clutter, but for us this was a good beginning.

Wednesday April 24

Although Canada is a bilingual country, it seems that many of our politicians are unable to converse in whichever of the languages is not their mother tongue. They would do well to use Claire Booth Luce's famous line when she was beginning a speech to a group of Italians.

"I am now going to try to talk to you in a language that is not mine, and when I do, you'll probably think it is not yours either!"

Thursday April 25

The first rule of wise financial management is to save something for a rainy day; the second, to distinguish between light sprinkles and heavy showers.

Friday April 26

    Thank God for friends, more prized as years
      increase.
    Let all else, if must be, cease;
    But, Lord of Life, I pray on me bestow
    The gifts of friends to share the way I go.

Thomas Curtis Clark

Saturday April 27

Although I am not usually one to bemoan the "good old days," my experience today left me wishing for just one more chance to speak with a "real" telephone operator.

How well I remember picking up my telephone and asking Helen to connect me with my sister Sarah, who was living in a small town some distance away. While she worked her magic, Helen and I would share pleasantries. "How's the family, Edna? I enjoyed George's sermon, on Sunday." "We're fine, Helen. See you at the picnic Wednesday." And then, "Good morning, Sarah." Mission accomplished.

A call to any large company was also a pleasure. Efficient receptionists would answer your call politely and connect you immediately to your party or, if that person was busy, find someone who could help you.

Today the call I placed was answered by a computer, "Good afternoon. Ms._____ is not at her desk. If you wish to leave a message, push one; if your call is urgent, push two." I pushed one. "Thank you. If you want Ms. _____ to return your call, push one, if you want to leave a message only, push two." I pushed one. "Thank you. For more efficient service, please enter you account number now." This command necessitated a frantic search through my papers, but alas, I was too slow. "I'm sorry, your number did not register. Please hang up and place this call again." Phooey!

Sunday April 28

Make a joyful noise unto God, all ye lands;
Sing forth unto the honour of his name;
make his praise glorious.
Come and see the works of God; [how
    wonderful] in
his doing towards the children of men.

Psalm 66:1, 2, 5

Monday April 29

Perfection consists not in doing extraordinary things, but in doing ordinary things extraordinarily well.

Antoine Arnauld

Tuesday April 30

My friend Will has a very dry wit. His wife, Muriel, likes to tell this story of their minor car accident to illustrate his sense of humour. Will and Muriel were stopped at a red light when their car was struck from behind by a somewhat flustered young lady.

"Pardon me, Miss," said Will as he got out to inspect the damage, "but how do you stop when I'm not here?"

May

Wednesday May 1

My daily wish is that we may
See good in those who pass our way:
Find in each a worthy trait
That we would gladly cultivate;
See in each one passing by
The better things that beautify—
A softly spoken word or cheer,
A kindly face, a smile sincere.

I pray each day that we might view
The things that warm one's heart anew:
The kindly deeds that can't be bought—
That only from the good are wrought,
A burden lightened here and there,
A brother lifted from despair,
The aged ones freed from distress,
The lame, the sick, brought happiness.

Grant that before each sun has set
We'll witness deeds we can't forget:
A soothing hand to one in pain,
A sacrifice for love—not gain;
A word to ease the troubled mind
Of one whose fate has seemed unkind.

So, friend, my wish is that we may
See good in all who pass our way.

My thanks to the unknown author

Thursday May 2

Sir Isaac Pitman, who developed the form of shorthand used for many years in offices all across North America, was also an advocate of spelling reform. Although shorthand became enormously popular, his phonetic spelling did not. He did, however, choose to use the spelling on his wife's tombstone. It reads:

In memori ov
Meri Pitman
Weif ov Eizac Pitman
Fonetic Printer, ov this site
Deid 19 Agust 1857
"Preper tu mit thei God."
Emos 4:12

Friday May 3

He who cannot forgive others breaks the bridge over which he must pass himself, for every man has need to be forgiven.

George Herbert

Saturday May 4

Dost thou love life? Then do not squander time, for that is the stuff life is made of.

Benjamin Franklin

Sunday May 5

He leadeth me, O blessed thought!
O words with heavenly comfort fraught!
What e're I do, where e're I be,
Still 'tis God's hand that leadeth me.

Joseph H. Gilmore

Monday May 6

As I was tidying a bookshelf today, I came across a work that I had nearly forgotten. *The Past is Precious* is a delightful volume that was published in Toronto a number of years ago. The story of its publication is very interesting.

A group of residents in a senior citizens' home worked together to publish a collection of poems, vignettes and other true stories, together with illustrations, that would be a record of their collective memories. Since the average age of the group was 86, this history would span nearly a century.

These energetic men and women successfully overcame many practical problems associated with the publication and, at the same time, managed to write their own contributions. The result was a delightful, very professional looking book full of wonderful stories about people and places of long ago. To the surprise of many, the book was sold out one week after publication.

What a loss to us all if these memories had been allowed to disappear. I look forward to rereading a book that is a tribute to a group of seniors who cared enough for the past to keep it fresh for us all.

Tuesday May 7

As I was doing my laundry today, I was feeling especially grateful for the technology that allows me to put clothes in a washing machine and then sit down to enjoy a cup of tea. So many of the household devices that we take for granted today were invented in the past 100 years. Here are just a few of the innovations that have made our lives better.

The mechanical washer was first produced in 1907 by the Maytag company, but it was 1937 before Bendix Aviation produced a fully automatic model.

Although a number of electric suction machines were being produced, one of the most effective ones was that of Murray Spangler, a night janitor. Made with goat-bristle brushes, a motor and a pillowcase to catch the dirt, his prototype became the first Hoover model vacuum cleaner in 1908.

Although it would be years before everyone could afford it, the Frigidaire (an electric refrigerator) was created in 1915.

The first licensed commercial radio station went on air in the 1920s, but it was not until 1939, when RCA came out with the first television, that our lives were irrevocably changed. We had news from around the world in our homes—as it was happening.

The microwave oven, as we know it today, became available in 1967, and the computer, once a 30-ton machine, can now be carried in a briefcase and is a large part of our daily lives. Ah progress!

Wednesday May 8

Flowers always make people better, happier and more helpful; they are sunshine, food and medicine to the soul.

Luther Burbank

Thursday May 9

A neighbour of ours, a nurse, often instructs pregnant women and their partners at Lamaze classes in the evening.

As well as giving information on the birth itself,

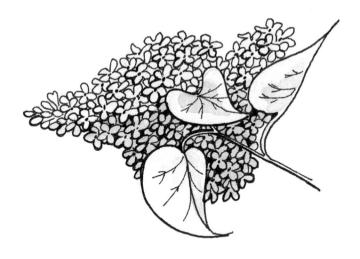

Sue often passes on helpful advice to the parents-to-be that she feels will make the birth process easier.

Last evening she announced, "You know ladies, exercise is very good for you and one of the best exercises is walking. And gentlemen, you could take time to walk with your partner. It would be good for you, too!" There was a brief moment of quiet and then a man's voice came from the middle of the group. "Would it be all right if she carries a golf bag while we walk?"

Friday May 10

Automation is a technological process that does all the work while you just sit there. When you were younger, this was called mother.

Saturday May 11

How the man plays the game shows something of his character; how he loses shows all of it.

Sunday May 12

Mother's Day

There is no slave out of heaven like a loving woman; and of all loving women, there is no such slave as a mother.

Henry Ward Beecher

God could not be everywhere and therefore he made mothers.

Jewish proverb

There is a religion in all deep love, but the love of a mother is the veil of a softer light between the heart and the heavenly Father.

Samuel Taylor Coleridge

Mother love is the fuel that enables a normal human being to do the impossible.

Marion C. Garretty

On this Mother's Day, I am especially grateful for the precious legacy my mother left me—an enduring love of family, home and friends.

Monday May 13

I went to our local nursing home today, hoping to take my dear friend Lila for a walk. Unfortunately, Lila has been under the weather for a few days and really wasn't up to being outdoors. Instead, we chose to go into the auditorium to hear a musical presentation from students at the middle school. It was a splendid choice!

Along with the choir, who sang several tunes in perfect harmony, there were a number of children who performed instrumental solos. One lad, who appeared to be among the youngest in the group, was one of the most gifted musicians I believe I have ever heard. This young man played the violin with an ability far beyond his years and his presentation moved many of the residents to tears. Seeing a youngster so talented with such passion for music left me feeling that the world will be a better place for his having been in it.

Tuesday May 14

To be a friend a man should strive to lift people up, to encourage and to set an example that will be an inspiration to others.

W. A. Peterson

Wednesday May 15

I particularly enjoyed these lines from Grace E. Easley. I hope you will, too.

Lord, Give Me Time

Lord, give me time to know a bit of peace,
Be free from care, before I grow too old.
Beyond the rainbow's end, may I at last,
Find where you've put my little pot of gold.
Lord, give me time to walk among the stars,
As fireflies flicker on a summer's night,
Feel the fragile snowflakes on my face,
Hold autumn to my heart in pure delight.

Lord, give me time to grow that I may fit
The mold of what you wish me to become.
It is not easy for me, casting off
These human failings that I suffer from.
But faith has eyes much clearer than my own,
And hope has wings to lift me up, and I'm
So full of Love, I know for sure I'm meant
For Heaven, given just a little time.

Thursday May 16

My son-in-law Bruce has begun his yearly pre-summer diet. "This year," he informed us, "I'm determined to fit into my shorts before summer arrives. I know I can shed these pounds quickly. After all, a diet is just a matter of mind over platter!"

Friday May 17

Treasure each other in the recognition that we do not know how long we shall have each other.

Joshua Loth Liebman

Saturday May 18

This is one of my favourite weekends of the year! In my childhood this holiday was kept on the actual birthday of Queen Victoria, May 24. When it was decided to move the holiday to the Monday preceding May 24, many cottagers took advantage of this extra day on the weekend to make their first of regular trips to the cottage. This has now become the traditional cottage-opening weekend and highways all across our country are choked with cars travelling to or from holiday properties.

Marg, Bruce and I have joined the many thousands here in Ontario who have travelled north to the Muskoka area. We are, once again, assisting my dear friend Eleanor with her cottage opening and enjoying the beauty of one of the province's most idyllic lake settings.

The dark water of the lake, the majesty of the tall pine trees, the beauty of the rocks and the haunting cries of the loons all combine to make days spent here some of the happiest of the year for me.

It's a beautiful world, this world of ours....

Sunday May 19

Stars of the evening, softly gleaming
In the fading West,
With your heavenly light is streaming
Hope to hearts opprest!
Toil is over, cease from sorrow,
'Til tomorrow
  Sleep and rest!

Mary Bradford Whiting

Monday May 20

Youth is a wonderful time of life when only the young are strong enough to endure.

These words crossed my mind today as I watched the youngsters next door make a mad dash into the lake. To me the water felt positively icy—certainly not warm enough to swim in. These young people have made this 24th-of-May weekend swim a ritual, and anyone who backs out of this chilly adventure suffers the sarcastic jibes of the rest of the group for the remainder of the season.

The enthusiasm of the young is a joy to behold!

Tuesday May 21

A friend thinks of you when all others are thinking of themselves.

Wednesday May 22

Bruce is making great effort to stick to his plan of weight loss. One of the meals he has enjoyed most often is Southern Chicken Salad with mustard dressing. Diet or not, this is a delicious dinner.

> 1 head romaine lettuce
> 3 cups cooked, shredded chicken
> 3/4 cup ripe olives, halved
> 1/3 cup sunflower seeds
> 1/4 cup whole green beans
> cherry tomatoes, sliced ripe olives and
>   sunflower seeds to garnish

Line a salad bowl with lettuce leaves. Shred the

remaining lettuce and put in the bowl. Combine chicken, olives, sunflower seeds and 1/2 cup mustard dressing (recipe below).

Heap the chicken mixture over the shredded lettuce. Steam the green beans until tender; drain. Arrange beans on top of the chicken salad. Garnish with cherry tomatoes, sliced ripe olives and sunflower seeds. Serve with extra dressing.

Mustard Dressing

Combine 1/3 cup white vinegar, 1 tbsp. Dijon mustard, 5 tbsp. sugar, 2 cloves garlic (minced), and 1/4 tsp. salt in a blender until smooth. Continue blending while slowly adding 1/2 cup vegetable oil until blended and dressing is thickened. Yield: 1 cup.

Thursday May 23

Lila Acheson Wallace, the Canadian-born co-founder of *Reader's Digest*, passed away in 1984 at the age of 94. Lila and her husband DeWitt compiled a fortune together, and together they gave much away.

She often said that she had memorized her will. It read, " I, Lila Acheson Wallace, being of sound mind and body... spent it."

Friday May 24

Readers frequently ask me if I find it difficult to do my writing every day. The answer, of course, is that some days the words come more easily than others, but persistence usually pays off.

The brilliant writer W. Somerset Maugham was once asked by a critic how he managed to write with such strict regularity, and complete his daily quota of writing.

"It's easy, my young friend," replied Maugham. "Each morning, write down the first word that occurs to you, then the next and the next, and so on. Don't worry if the words appear to have no connection. This is simply an exercise to warm up the mind. What you write will gradually take on meaning and, before you know it, you're in the middle of the job."

Saturday May 25

The man with a new idea is a crank until the idea succeeds.

Mark Twain

Sunday May 26

All things bright and beautiful
All creatures great and small,

All things wise and wonderful—
The Lord God made them all.

Cecil Francis Alexander

Monday May 27

Memorial Day in the United States is the day set aside each year to honour loved ones who have passed away. Originally intended to honour those who died in service of their country, it has become a day of remembrance for all who have gone beyond.

The tributes offered on this day are made from the memories we cherish of loved ones all the years of our lives.

One of the most moving tributes I have read was written by William Allen White following the accidental death of his 17-year-old daughter, Mary. In his eulogy, Mr. White reviews Mary's life and activities, finishing with an expression of faith in eternal life.

"A rift in the clouds on a gray day threw a shaft of sunlight on her coffin as her nervous, energetic little body sank to its last sleep. But the soul of her, the glowing, gorgeous, fervent soul of her, surely was flaming in eager joy upon some other dawn."

Tuesday May 28

The test of a first-rate intelligence is the ability to hold two opposed ideas in mind at the same time and still retain the ability to function. One should, for example, be able to see that things are hopeless and yet be determined to make them otherwise.

F. Scott Fitzgerald

Wednesday May 29

A truly rich man is one whose children run into his arms when his hands are empty.

Thursday May 30

No one so thoroughly appreciates the value of constructive criticism as the one who's giving it.

Hal Chadwick

Friday May 31

Things turn out for the best for the people who make the best of the way things turn out.

Art Linkletter

June

Saturday June 1

This is the day of gratitude for me as it is the anniversary of my wedding day. I am so grateful for my dear husband, George, and the years of happiness that we shared together. I am thankful for our three daughters, our grandchildren and our great-grandchildren.

I miss my beloved husband very much, but I will continue to celebrate this day with much joy and a grateful heart for all of my blessings.

Sunday June 2

Little drops of water,
Little grains of sand,
Make the mighty ocean
And the beauteous land.

And the little moments,
Humble though they be,
Make the mighty ages,
Of eternity.

Julia A. Carney

Monday June 3

Good friends of Mary and John are moving to British Columbia. Although they enjoy that beautiful province, they will miss their home and friends that they are leaving behind. I was reminded of a letter that I received many years ago from dear friends, Mary and Gerald Harding, when they moved after many years in the same home.

"You know, Edna, I am so very happy that Gerald and I will be moving by the sea once more. There is nothing quite so nice as hearing the call of the gulls or the wash of the waves on the beach. Gerald and I are most anxious to be near the ocean once more.

"But there is something about having strangers moving through our home, looking into our rooms. I want to tell them about the good times, the laughter and the joy these rooms have seen. I long to have them share the memories that are held here. They want to talk about the rugs and the storm windows."

I'm sure Mary and John's friends share these same thoughts.

Tuesday June 4

Sir Arthur Conan Doyle, creator of the famous Sherlock Holmes, was a great lover of our country, as he showed in the following excerpt from "The Athabasca Trail."

My life is gliding downward, it speeds
swifter to the day
When it shoots the last dark canyon
to the Plains of Faraway;
But while its streams are running
through the years that are to be,
The mighty voice of Canada will ever call to
me.

Wednesday June 5

The glory of friendship is not the outstretched hand, nor the kindly smile, nor the joy of companionship; it is the spiritual inspiration that comes to one when he discovers that someone else believes in him and is willing to trust him with his friendship.

Ralph Waldo Emerson

Thursday June 6

I enjoyed these words of Louis Nizer:

"A man who works with his hands and his brain is a craftsman; a man who works with his hands and his brain and his heart is an artist."

Friday June 7

The month of June has long been a particular favourite of mine. The grass is green, the flowers are blooming, the sun shines warmly, but the heavy heat of summer is not yet upon us.

Lila McGuinness and I spent some time in the garden today enjoying the fragrance of the lily of the valley, now in bloom. My husband, George, often brought me bouquets of this fragrant flower, and I can feel 25 years old just by closing my eyes and breathing in the lovely perfume. Lila and I picked several stalks to bring indoors. We both find it quite amazing that such tiny flowers should have an aroma that is so powerful.

The lily of the valley is as old as the Bible. How strange it is to think that the people of biblical times enjoyed many of the same flowers that we do today. It somehow makes it easier to think of them as real people when I read, "I am the rose of Sharon, and the lily of the valleys" in the Song of Solomon.

June truly is a month for beautiful flowers and lovely days to share with good friends.

Saturday June 8

Advice is like snow; the softer it falls, the longer it dwells upon, and the deeper it sinks into, the mind.

Samuel Taylor Coleridge

Sunday June 9

For flowers that bloom about our feet,
For tender grass so fresh and sweet,
For song of bird and hum of bee,
For all things fair we hear and see,
Father in heaven we thank Thee.

Ralph Waldo Emerson

Monday June 10

Yesterday was my birthday. My, how quickly it seems to come each year! I enjoy these thoughts from Seneca as I move forward, ever more quickly, into my "golden years."

"As for old age, embrace and love it. It abounds with pleasure if you know how to use it. The gradually (I do not say rapidly) declining years are amongst the sweetest in a man's life; and I maintain, that even where they have reached the extreme limit, they have their pleasure still."

Tuesday June 11

In the times of quietness, our hearts should be like trees, lifting their branches to the sky to draw down strength which they will need to face the storms that will surely come.

Toyokiko Kagawa

Wednesday June 12

I always enjoyed the humour of Mark Twain and this story is a particular favourite.

Mark Twain was invited by the artist Whistler to see a new painting that was nearly finished. Twain studied the picture for some time and then said, "I would do away with that cloud, if I were you." As he spoke, he waved his hand toward the offending cloud.

"Gad sir," said Whistler, "Please be careful! The paint is not yet dry."

"Oh, don't worry," Twain replied, "I have my gloves on."

Thursday June 13

Crab Apple Tree in Bloom

In all the world there is no lovelier thing
Than this wild crab tree on a sunny hill!
Its pink-white glory, strangely startling,
The windless day is suddenly so still—

I dare not breathe lest I should shatter quite
This radiant mass of colour and light.

I dare not touch one little clustered spray
Lest some wild bee from out a blossom's heart
Should take his heavy–bodied, bungling way,
And the delicate shaken petals fall apart.

O wind, be kind! O bees, in hurrying past,
Go softly that this loveliness may last.

Grace Noll Crowell

Friday June 14

Consider how hard it is to change yourself and you'll understand what little chance you have of trying to change others.

Saturday June 15

I know my husband, George, would have been surprised to know that I have become a baseball fan. I also enjoy interesting baseball stories. Today's anecdote comes from my grandson Marshall.

When Bill Veeck was the president of the Chicago White Sox, he created a new scoreboard. It looked like a usual scoreboard until the time that a Chicago player hit a home run.

As the ball soared out of sight, coloured fireworks flew out of the top of the scoreboard in a loud and dazzling display. As if this were not enough, coloured lights played up and down the sides of the board, while horns honked, whistles tooted and sirens screamed. All of this happened only when Chicago scored.

Casey Stengel, then manager of the New York Yankees, finally struck back. During a night game, one of the Yankee players hit a home run. The scoreboard was silent. At a nod from Coach Stengel, the entire Yankee team marched out of the dugout and turned to face the crowd. On

Stengel's next signal, every player pulled out a sparkler, lit it and waved it with unbridled enthusiasm at the silent crowd.

Sunday June 16

Father's Day

What is the gift you will give your boy?
A glamorous game, a tinseled toy,
A whittling knife, a puzzle pack,
A train that runs on a curving track,
A boy scout book, a real live pet?
No, there's plenty of time for such things yet.
Give him a day for his very own,
Just your boy and his dad alone;
A walk in the woods, a game in the park,
A fishing trip from dawn to dark.

Give him the gift that only you can,
The companionship of his "old man."
Games are outgrown and toys decay,
But he'll never forget if you give him a day.

Author unknown

Monday June 17

Life is no brief candle to me. It is a sort of splendid torch which I have got hold of for the moment, and I want to make it burn as brightly as possible before handing it over to future generations.

George Bernard Shaw

Tuesday June 18

Our health is something that most of us take for granted. As we grow older, we begin to "wear out," and it becomes increasingly important to maintain a lifestyle conducive to good health.

"Eating wisely, exercising and getting enough rest," says one family doctor, "are probably the best ways that an older person has of enjoying his days fully."

When we are younger, a meal skipped or a few hours of sleep missed don't seem to affect us. As a person get older, these things can have a more detrimental effect on both the mind and the body.

I appreciate Isaak Walton's thoughts on health:

"Look to your health; and if you have it, praise God and value it next to a good conscience; for health is the second blessing that we mortals are capable of—a blessing that money cannot buy; therefore value it, and be thankful for it."

SHELL COLLECTOR

Wednesday June 19

The rung of a ladder was never meant to rest upon, but only to hold a man's foot long enough to enable him to put the other somewhat higher.

Thomas Henry Huxley

Thursday June 20

The dictionary defines an optimist as "one who takes the most hopeful view of matters." I have always been a optimistic person, as are many of my friends. Today I offer several thoughts about optimism.

When it is dark enough, you can see the stars.

Charles Beard

Optimism is the belief that even when worst comes to worst, it won't be so bad.

An optimist is a fellow who believes what will be will be postponed

Ken Hubbard

The habit of looking on the bright side of every event is worth more than a thousand pounds a year.

Samuel Johnson

Remember the teakettle: when it's up to its neck in hot water, it sings.

My grandmother

What is optimism?
To look up and not down
To look forward and not back,
To look out and not in, and to
lend a hand.

E. E. Hale

Friday June 21

Today marks the arrival of our summer season. I found these lines from Garnett Ann Schultz to be a fine way to start this lovely time of the year.

One Golden Gift

God sends to us one golden gift,
It starts with one bright dawn;
The darkness quickly fades to light
And nighttime then is gone.
Enchantment fills our heart with joy;
We hear the singing birds;
In hush and quietness we wait,
No need for human words.

God wraps the day in one blue sky
Atop the world so bright:

A carpet soft in summer's world,
The green grass of delight.
The rolling hills and singing streams,
A shaded lane of bliss;
As fleecy clouds go floating by—
No thrill is quite like this.

God bids the world to come awake
As sleeping meadows sigh:
Within the laughter of the dawn
We watch a butterfly
And honeybees, buzzing there
Amidst the clover's bloom.
One golden gift—this summer day
With all the world in tune.

Saturday June 22

Summer is a time for backyard barbeques, and dining alfresco. My son-in-law Bruce is an excellent chef who really enjoys using the grill. I hope you will like Bruce's recipe.

Grilled Pepper Cheese Steaks

3/4 cup diced onions
1 small green pepper, finely chopped
1 small sweet red pepper, finely chopped
2 cloves garlic
1 tbsp. vegetable oil
1/2 cup shredded Monterey Jack cheese

1/2 cup Italian-seasoned bread crumbs
6 (4 oz.) beef tenderloin steaks, 1 1/2 inches
   thick

Heat oil in a non-stick skillet. Sauté the onions,
peppers and garlic in the hot oil until tender.

Remove from heat and stir in cheese and bread
crumbs until well mixed.

Cut a pocket into each steak; spoon pepper and
cheese mixture into the steak pockets. Secure
with wooden toothpicks.

Grill, with lid closed, over medium high heat
(350–400°F) 10 to 15 minutes or until steak is
cooked as you desire it. Serves 6.

Bruce's tips for grilling:

1. To prevent burns, open a covered grill
   slowly and carefully to allow hot air and
   steam to escape.
2. Use long-handled grilling tools.
3. Use a spray bottle of water to put out flare-
   ups on a charcoal grill.
4. Do not wear loose clothing that could catch
   fire when you are grilling.
5. Turn foods with tongs or a spatula to avoid
   piercing meat and losing juices.
6. Brush hot rack with a stiff wire brush after
   each use.

Sunday June 23

I need not show my faith. Thrice eloquent
Are quiet trees and the green listening sod;
Hushed are the stars, whose power is never
    spent;
The hills are mute: yet how they speak of God!

Charles Hanson Towne

Monday June 24

This is a day of celebration in the province of Quebec and in other French-speaking communities across Canada. St. Jean Baptiste Day is often observed by attending an early morning mass, after which families gather together for a traditional Quebecois dinner of tourtière.

How well I remember the many times that George and I spent St. Jean Baptiste Day with our good friends Paul and Madeleine Pouliot and their wonderful large family. These delightful people celebrated their French-Canadian background with great enthusiasm! How lucky we are to have such diverse cultures within the confines of one country.

Tuesday June 25

When people tell you how young you look, they are also telling you how old you are.

Wednesday June 26

As the school year draws to a close, I can't help but marvel at the skill and dedication of the teachers who have made the learning experience such a joyful one for their students.

Many people are under the mistaken impression that the job of teaching is an easy one. For those people I would like to suggest that they spend just one day in a classroom. I feel sure that by the end of that day they would see a teacher for what he or she is—a wonderfully patient, caring, hard-working person who deserves the respect of us all.

Thank you to all the teachers for the wonderful job that you do!

Thursday June 27

My granddaughter Phyllis amused us with this anecdote.

A man at a party said to the fellow next to him, "It's very dull here, isn't it?"

"Yes, very," said the man.

"Well then, let's go home."

"Gosh, I'm afraid that I can't leave. I'm the host."

Friday June 28

It takes a long time to become young.

Pablo Picasso

Saturday June 29

Good friends of Marg and Bruce are faced with a very difficult decision. Jack's mother, who has had some memory problems in the past, seems now to be incapable of taking care of herself. Jack and Jenny must now find a place where Gwen will be well cared for until her days here on earth are ended. This is an enormous responsibility—one which Jack and Jenny are finding challenging.

Fortunately, help is available to them through the local health service and they have spent many hours visiting the different long-term facilities searching for the one they feel will best suit Gwen's needs.

Although none of us wants to have our roles reversed, when a parent becomes the child and the child the parent, it sometimes happens. When it does, one would hope for children who are as loving and caring as Jack and Jenny.

Sunday June 30

My times are in my Father's hand:
How could I wish or ask for more?
For He who has my pathway planned
Will guide me till my journey's o'er.

Fraser

July

Monday July 1
"Oh Canada, our home and native land."

I am extremely proud to be a Canadian and I think that pride and loyalty to this land are very important to the health and strength of the nation.

Our hope for the future depends on all of us joining together and working towards a common goal of unity and strength. Only by doing this will we continue to be the "true North strong and free." Sir John A. Macdonald said, "Whatever you do, adhere to the Union—we are a great country, and shall become one of the greatest in the universe if we preserve it; we shall sink into insignificance and adversity if we suffer it to be broken."

Tuesday July 2
We love old cathedrals, old furniture, old silver, old dictionaries and old prints, but we have entirely forgotten about the beauty of old men. I think an appreciation of that kind of

beauty is essential to our life; for beauty, it seems to me, is what is old and mellow and well smoked.

Lin Yutang

Wednesday July 3

Don't believe the world owes you a living; the world owes you nothing—it was here first.

Robert J. Burdette

Thursday July 4

Today our neighbours to the south are celebrating Independence Day. The "Glorious Fourth" for Americans is a day of inspiration and renewal—a day to enjoy the "inalienable right to the pursuit of happiness." I offer Edna Jaques's "Building A Nation" in their honour.

It isn't battlefields and guns
that make a nation great,
Or clanking arms or marching men
  or panoply of state.
It isn't pageantry or power
  where might and triumph ride,
For kingdoms are not built on war
  or nations fed on pride.

It's the little homes against the earth
  where peace and love abide,

It's rugged hills and quiet fields
    across the countryside.
It's children trudging off to school
    secure and clean and gay,
Who own the right to childhood
    the right to laugh and play.
It's stony fields and little brooks
    with hidden age-old springs,
It's tender songs of youth and love
    that someone's mother sings,
It's love of home and firelight
    it's sweat and faith and toil—
The souls of men who earn their bread
    from sun and rain and soil.

It's something deeper still than this,
    beyond our heart and ken,
A faith that sees the good that lies
    within the hearts of men.
A woman glad to bear a child
    protected by her mate,
It's home and love and family
    that makes a nation great.

Friday July 5

Here in Canada, the drive-in movie is nearly a thing of the past. Only in some of the smaller communities are the once-popular theatres still open during the warm summer evenings.

How well I remember Marg and Bruce putting Phyllis and Marshall into their pyjamas, piling into the car and, while the youngsters slept in the back, enjoying an evening's entertainment—without the cost of a babysitter.

Drive-in theatres were not only found in North America, however. In many countries around the world, young and old alike were attracted to these open-air cinemas. There were some rather unusual regulations at a drive-in in a small village in India. The notice on the wall warned: "Viewing the show from beyond the boundary of the walls by sitting on a camel or on a nearby tree is strictly prohibited. Additionally, the management cannot be held responsible in the event that a viewer is bitten by a scorpion or a snake."

Saturday July 6

You have not lived a perfect day unless you have done something for someone who will never be able to repay you.

Ruth Smeltzer

Sunday July 7

Teach me, O Lord, the way to thy statutes; and I shall keep it unto the end.

Give me understanding, and I shall keep thy law; yea, I shall observe it with my whole heart.

Psalm 119: 33–34

Monday July 8

When grace is joined with wrinkles, it is adorable. There is an unspeakable dawn in happy old age.

Victor Hugo

Tuesday July 9

This is a day that has doubly blessed our family. Phyllis and Bill commemorate their anniversary and their twins, Justin and Jenny, celebrate their seventeenth birthday. It scarcely seems possible that it was 17 years ago we stood in the hospital and viewed these two tiny perfect little beings. And here they are today, about to enter their final year of high school and thinking about university. At the risk of using a well-worn cliché, Where has the time gone?

I am so proud of my grandchildren and great-grandchildren. They are fine people and a tribute to our family.

Dr. Benjamin Spock observed, "The best upbringing children can receive is to observe their parents taking excellent care of themselves—mind, body, spirit. Children, being the world's greatest mimics, naturally and automatically model their parents' behaviour."

Wednesday July 10

How I love the roses that grow so profusely in our garden. This year we have one particularly beautiful bush whose colour is a shade of peach that I have rarely seen. My friend June Ragwell gave me a recipe for rose potpourri that was taken from a diary kept by the wife of a nineteenth-century sea captain. It is possible that I have given this recipe before, but I believe it is worth sharing again.

Ingredients: A Chinese jar, an apron full of rose petals, a handful of salt, 2 oz. whole allspice, 2 oz. stick cinnamon (broken into pieces), 1 oz orris root (bruised and broken), 2 oz. lavender flowers, 8 drops oil of rose, 1/4 pint cologne (the best you can afford).

Directions: Gather the roses when all the dew is gone. Separate the petals and let them dry. Then scatter them in a large covered dish and sprinkle each layer with salt. Stir every morning for 10 days. Let them stand for six weeks in a covered fruit jar with the allspice and cinnamon at the bottom. When you put them in the Chinese jar, add the orris root, the lavender, the rose oil and the cologne.

A proper potpourri will last for years and years. All you have to do is add a little lavender or rose oil whenever you wish—and cologne when you can spare it.

Thursday July 11

For many years summer was a time for sun worshippers to spend hours lying in the sun and working hard to turn their skin a dark brown. The tanned look was thought to look healthy and glamorous.

More recently, doctors have made us aware of the effect that the sun's ultraviolet rays have on our skin. Prolonged exposure to the sun, particularly between the hours of noon and two o'clock in the afternoon, causes premature aging and certain types of cancer.

Fortunately, scientists have developed sunscreens or sun blocks that help protect our skin from the sun's rays.

The SPF (or sun-protection-factor) ratings on sunscreens give a method for determining the amount of protection each lotion will give. Dermatologists suggest that SPF 15 is the lowest number that should be worn on skin exposed to the sun; in summer, SPF 45 is highly recommended.

Although all of us should be aware of the effects of the sun's rays, parents should be particularly cautious of their children's exposure and make sure that youngsters are never outdoors without wearing sunscreen. As the old adage says, "An ounce of prevention is worth a pound of cure."

Friday July 12

Conscience takes up more room than all the rest of a person's insides.

Mark Twain

Saturday July 13

Every year at this time, with the blackflies finally gone, I like to get out our well-loved picnic basket and plan an outing with the family.

My picnic basket has been in the family for many years, and holds memories of lunches from one coast of our great country to the other. The basket itself is made from white ash with a hinged top and it is a handsome, sturdy affair, roomy enough to carry the fixings for a big picnic.

When planning a picnic, a most important thing to bring is a picnic blanket. I have found that a very large, machine-washable, all-cotton throw of medium weight is indispensable. This blanket may be used as a tablecloth as often as a throw, so I choose one that is multi-coloured and patterned (spills will show less). I also like to use cloth napkins, although paper napkins may be more practical, particularly if there are children with you.

Over the years, I have collected a wide variety of coloured dishes, cups and cutlery which give our picnics a very festive look.

When packing your picnic basket, it's important to make sure that any food items that need to be chilled have plenty of ice packed around them. We usually use plastic containers for food and we pack them into a larger plastic tub with ice.

With your basket and good friends or family members bundled into the car, you are ready for a wonderful outing on a beautiful summer day.

Sunday July 14

> Summer suns are glowing over land and sea
> Happy light is flowing bountiful and free,
> Everything rejoices in the mellow rays,
> All earth's thousand voices swell the song of
>   praise.
> God's mercy streameth over all the world,
> And His banner gleameth, everywhere
>   unfurled.
> Broad and deep and glorious as the heaven
>   above
> Shines in might victorious His eternal love.

Bishop Walsham How

Monday July 15

One of the most enjoyable things about summer is the chance to spend time with the neighbourhood children. When the youngsters are at school their opportunities to visit are infrequent. Now that summer holidays are here, many of the boys and girls stop by to chat with me on a regular basis. How much I enjoy listening to their thoughts and views on our world today. Many times their ideas are very profound and I am often surprised by the depth of their interest in—and knowledge of—not only our country, but the rest of the world. Television and computers have put the young people of today in touch with the far corners of the earth. "What a small world" has taken on a whole new meaning.

Tuesday July 16

My grandson Marshall and his wife, Jamie, along with their children, Bethany and Michael, have become very interested in sailing. When he was younger, Marshall would often crew for good friends and these young people would spend weekends racing at yacht-club regattas. His interest in sailing has remained constant and he and his family have purchased a sailboat that will sleep four people and, with the other amenities on board, will allow them to spend weekends and holidays enjoying the breezes on Lake Ontario. Marshall and Jamie hope that their children will learn to love the slow and easy pace that sailing provides in a world that seems to be moving at a whirlwind speed.

I laughed when Marshall read me this thought from Lin and Larry Pardey.

"No amount of skill, no equipment and no boat will keep you from disaster if you don't develop the most important seagoing skill of all: a complete fear of falling overboard."

Wednesday July 17

The great thing about getting older is that you don't lose all the other ages that you have been.

Madeleine L'Engle

Thursday July 18

If you tell a man there are 300 billion stars in the universe, he will believe you. But if you tell him a bench has just been painted, he has to touch it to be sure.

Friday July 19

This evening we had a barbecue dinner at my grandson Fred's home. He and his wife, June, their children, Mickey and Geoffrey, and a large group of their neighbours took advantage of a beautiful summer evening to get together and enjoy a dinner and a spectacular show of stars in the dark night sky.

For dessert, June had platters of icy watermelon slices. My first bite brought back a wonderful memory almost forgotten.

When I was a child my mother made pickles of all kinds. One day each summer, Mother would invite all of the children in our neighbourhood over to our home. She would wait for a particularly hot and humid day when she knew that icy cold watermelon would be a very welcome treat.

We kids would spend the afternoon devouring slice after slice of the sweet fruit and then we'd have seed-spitting contests on the lawn.

Later, mother would collect all of our rinds and for the next few days she would make watermelon pickles to be enjoyed over the fall and winter.

Ah, the memories!

Saturday July 20

On July 20, 1969, astronaut Neil Armstrong took "one small step for man, one giant leap for mankind," when he stepped onto the surface of the moon.

What an incredible experience it must have been for Armstrong and fellow astronaut Edwin "Buzz" Aldrin to be the first humans on the moon! For those of us watching it on television back here on earth, the feat seemed almost surreal.

Although there are many moons and stars left to conquer, we live in a time of technological and scientific development where very little seems impossible. But no matter where science will lead us in the years to come, it is unlikely that that "one small step" will ever be forgotten.

Sunday July 21

When I consider thy heavens, the work of thy fingers, the moon and the stars, which thou hast ordained;

What is man, that thou art mindful of him? And the son of man, that thou visitest him?

Psalm 8: 3–4

Monday July 22

Genius is nothing but a great aptitude for patience.

Benjamin Franklin

Tuesday July 23

In a day and age when divorce is at an all-time high and society seems to have taken separations and marital breakups for granted, I am delighted to be sharing Bruce and Margaret's wedding anniversary. Being happily married for many years takes much work and commitment on both sides. Thankfully, Marg and Bruce have put the effort needed into their life together and we look forward to a wonderful family celebration of their marriage this evening. As a tribute to their ongoing love, I offer a number of thoughts on love and marriage.

Love does not consist in gazing at each other, but in looking together in the same direction.
Antoine de Saint-Exupéry

If you want to be loved, be lovable.
Ovid

No strong marriage can be founded on "We'll see how long we can make it last," only on "We will make it last long."
Jenny de Vries

A happy marriage is a long conversation that always seems too short.
André Maurois

The keystone to any marriage is one word, "WE."
Pam Brown

Wednesday July 24

Sing a song of summer, the world is nearly still,
The millpond has gone to sleep, and so has the mill.
Shall we go a sailing, or shall we take a ride,
Or dream the afternoon away here, side by side?
Cosmo Monkhouse

Thursday July 25

I received a lovely postcard today from my friend Emily, who is travelling in Spain. Pictured on the front was a small villa on a hillside surrounded by magnificent flowers. It wasn't hard for me to imagine Emily sitting inside the villa, sipping iced tea and enjoying the view.

Emily knows that I have collected postcards for many years and she sends me cards from her many yearly travels.

Deltiology, the collecting of postcards, is becoming a hobby for many people here in Canada.

Many of the most interesting cards date back to the turn of the twentieth century. They often picture local subjects or landmarks that no longer exist. These early cards are sometimes the only pictorial record of main streets, monuments or historical sites that have disappeared.

Old postcards may be found at flea markets or in antique shops and collecting them can be a very enjoyable pastime.

Friday July 26

I have noticed over the years that our world has become much noisier. There is very little silence in our lives and I, for one, really miss it.

We live in a world of roaring jet engines, jackhammers, and the unavoidable noise of truck engines, car horns and other sounds that assail our ears.

People need silence. Silence encourages us to think and to appreciate the world around us.

The philosopher Schopenhauer once said that noise "paralyzes the brain, murders thought and must cause pain to anyone who has anything like an idea in his head."

Saturday July 27

Nature gives to every time and season some beauties of its own; and from morning to night, as from the cradle to the grave, is but a succession of changes so gentle and easy that we can scarcely mark their progress.

Charles Dickens

Sunday July 28

This is my Father's world,
And to my listening ears
All nature sings, and round me rings
The music of the spheres.

Maltbie Davenport Babcock

Monday July 29

Be cheerful. Of all things you wear, your expression is the most important.

Tuesday July 30

When you stop loving someone, it is easy to understand that the love is ended. When someone stops loving you, it takes a long time before you are sure that that person won't have a change of heart.

Wednesday July 31

Write it on your heart that every day is the best day in the year. He is rich who owns the day, and no one owns the day who allows it to be invaded with fret and worry and anxiety. Finish every day and be done with it. You have done what you could. Some blunders and absurdities no doubt crept in; forget them as soon as you can.

Tomorrow is a new day; begin it well and serenely and with too high a spirit to be cumbered with your old nonsense.

This new day is all that is good and fair. It is too dear, with its hopes and invitations, to waste a moment on yesterday.

Ralph Waldo Emerson

SUMMER VACATION

August

Thursday August 1

I so love the summer months—the warm sun, the beautiful flowers, starlit skies and hours spent outdoors in the company of friends and family. As we begin this month, these lovely lines from Molly Elaine Johnson seem to feed my spirit.

Summer is a Smile

Summer is a smile, broad, unrestrained,
A heartfelt smile, so warm, unfeigned.
The teeming earth beneath its glow
Breathes and responds, and row on row,
Blossoms nod their genial heads
And stretch their toes in earthen beds.

This smile of summer, golden spun,
I've found in sweet strains from the sun,
In the warmth of sod, the grinning trees,
And the friendly touch of a gentle breeze,
In the thick woods with finches of gold and
   black.
Summer just makes you smile back.

Friday August 2

There is a serene and settled majesty to woodland scenery that enters into the soul and delights and elevates it, and fills it with noble inclinations.

Washington Irving

Saturday August 3

My brother-in-law Ben and his wife, Marie, recently returned from a trip to Montreal. Rather than taking Highway 401, they chose to drive back roads and found a rather unique piece of Ontario history.

About 40 kilometres northeast of Cornwall are the magnificent ruins of the St. Raphael Cathedral. The history of the cathedral is very interesting. In 1784, at the conclusion of the Revolutionary War in the United States, those who fought for England were given land grants. These men, mostly of Highland Scots origin, found their land in Charlottenburg Township on the banks of the Raisin River in Ontario.

Two years later, some 500 more Scots arrived here, led by Alexander MacDonnell, their parish priest. The parish grew quickly, and under the leadership of the second Father MacDonnell (the first father having passed away in 1803), this parish, St. Raphael, became the administrative centre of the Catholic church in Upper Canada. In 1821 construction began on a majestic stone cathedral.

The magnificent cathedral was a focus in the community until 1970 when a fire raced through the church, leaving nothing but the walls standing. Parishioners decided to leave the ruin just as it was and even today services and plays take place in the building that is open to the heavens.

Ben and Marie enjoyed their visit to this unusual and beautiful cathedral that has a place in our cultural heritage.

Sunday August 4

Be strong and of a good courage; be not afraid, neither be thou dismayed: for the Lord thy God is with thee whithersoever thou goest.

Joshua 1:9

Monday August 5

Summer desserts can be simple, delicious and easy to make. Here is a fruit dessert that looks as good as it tastes. Cantaloupe boats are a festive ending for any special dinner.

Cantaloupe Boats
1/2 lb. green seedless grapes
1/4 cup sugar
1 egg white, slightly beaten
1 large cantaloupe

6 lime wedges
6 mint sprigs

Break or cut washed grapes into 6 clusters.
Dip in egg white, then in sugar, coating well.
Place on waxed paper to dry.
Cut cantaloupe into 6 wedges; scoop out seeds.
Top each wedge with a cluster of frosted grapes; garnish with a lime wedge and sprig of mint. Serves 6.

Tuesday August 6

Marg, Bruce and I spent yesterday, the Civic Holiday, with Jamie, Marshall and their children on the sailboat in Lake Ontario. What a glorious time we had!

Marshall is a skilled yachtsman and we fairly skimmed across the water, tacking back and forth as we made our way towards Port Credit. There we enjoyed a wonderful lunch at the yacht club before heading back towards a berth at a small harbour just east of Toronto.

It was a marvelous way to spend a summer's day. I feel so lucky to have had this time on the water.

These words come from Herb Payson:

"Sailing does this for me! The world leaps into my eyes and ears, touches me in private places, and afterwards, I return to the mainstream of my life renewed."

Wednesday August 7

> One ship sails East
>   And another sails West
> By the self-same winds that blow.
>   It's the set of the sails
> And not the gales
>   That determines which way they go.

Anonymous

Thursday August 8

My friend Jake made me laugh today when he read me this list:

You know you are getting older when—
You get winded playing checkers,
Everything hurts and what doesn't hurt, doesn't work,
You look forward to a dull evening,
You have too much room in your house, and not enough in the medicine chest,
You need your glasses to find your glasses.
You need a fire permit to light all your birthday candles and you need oxygen after you blow them out.

Friday August 9

My great-grandson Geoffrey drove me to Muskoka today for my yearly visit with my dear friend Eleanor. Geoffrey was going north to visit some friends at their family cottage so he asked if I would like to ride with him. We spent a wonderful two hours talking and remembering many happy family occasions. I did have to laugh several times when he prefaced his remarks with "Do you remember when I was young...?"

Saturday August 10

James Herriot, the British author who wrote of his adventures as a vet, explained how he came to write his best-selling series of books.

"I kept telling my wife for 25 years that I was going to write a book, but she didn't think I would. Then one day she said to me, 'We had our silver anniversary last week, and you're 50; you'll never do it now.' So I thought, okay mate, I will."

He frequently typed in front of his television set in the evenings and it was there that he found his *nom de plume* (British veterinarian etiquette required a pen-name, as authorship could be construed as self-advertisement). He chose the name James Herriot from the goalkeeper of a soccer team he was watching on television as he tapped out his manuscript.

Although Herriot passed away several years

ago, his books remain immensely popular with young and old alike. Anyone who has never enjoyed these humourous recollections has truly missed some gems.

Sunday August 11

Abide with me, fast falls the eventide;
The darkness deepens; Lord with me abide:
When other helpers fail and comforts flee,
Help of the helpless, oh abide with me!

Henry F. Lyte

Monday August 12

How happy I am to be here in Muskoka with Eleanor. This is such a beautiful area of Ontario, and it seems that each time I am here, I learn something that I previously knew nothing about.

This morning we watched as the steamship *Segwun* passed by the end of the dock. This beautiful old boat is the last of what was a large fleet of steamers in the Muskoka Lakes Navigation and Hotel Company that served lakes Muskoka, Rosseau and Joseph in the early 1900s. On a boat cruise yesterday, we passed by Keewaydin Island where another of these steamers, the *Waome*, sunk on the morning of October 6, 1934. Of course nothing can be seen from the surface, but

I was interested to read of the storm that took this ship to the bottom with the loss of three lives.

The *Waome* (Ojibway for water lily) came out of the Indian River heading for Bracebridge in light winds and calm water. A savage storm, possibly a water spout, came suddenly and hit the boat off the starboard stern. The vessel rolled on her port side, throwing the captain and four others into the icy water. Two others, trapped in the passenger lounge, were carried to a watery grave as the vessel sank, probably less than a minute after the storm struck.

The *Waome* righted herself on the way to the bottom and now sits on the floor of the lake about 70 feet below the surface.

The sinking of the *Waome* remains one of the great tragedies on Lake Muskoka.

Tuesday August 13

August is a plump, cream-fed cat, purring in the sun. The frantic energy of the growing season has slackened; the dress rehearsals of early summer are over; August is what summer has been aiming for. There is a truce now with lawn and lawnmower, with weeds and crabgrass, with undone tasks, with energy and activity. Now, in August, there is time and licence to sit and listen to deep summer.

Betty Volk

Wednesday August 14

Sitting outside this evening, Eleanor and I were treated to a spectacular display.

As the sun set and the stars came out, we sat quietly on the dock enjoying the beautiful evening. As we watched, the northern sky came alive with beams of light, silvery blue at first, and then as they became stronger, a multitude of colours. The *aurora borealis*, or northern lights as they are known, is a phenomenon seen in the northern sky. These ribbons of light are actually a glow from atoms and molecules in the earth's upper atmosphere.

We watched, fascinated as the lights danced in the sky. When we finally went into the cottage, we felt as though we had briefly glimpsed the beauty of eternity.

Thursday August 15

The measure of one's success is not the wealth accumulated, the shrines erected, the records broken, or the battles won. It is the inner strength which builds each day through hard work, integrity, and a respect for mankind.

Melvin Simon

Friday August 16

The block of granite, which is an obstacle in the pathway of the weak, becomes a stepping stone for the strong.

Thomas Carlyle

Saturday August 17

Have courage for the great sorrows of life and patience with the small ones; and when you have labouriously accomplished your daily task, go to sleep in peace.

God is awake.

Victor Hugo

Sunday August 18

Let the words of my mouth, and the meditation of my heart, be acceptable in thy sight, O Lord, my strength and my redeemer.

Psalm 19:14

Monday August 19

Many cottagers here in the Muskoka area are from the United States. I was interested to learn how one of these American families happened to choose Muskoka for their summer home.

Elsie and Henry Hillman, from Pittsburgh, Pennsylvania, have been coming to the Beaumaris area for many years. Elsie explained a bit of the background of their cottage, called "Ramatola," and of their family's long history in Muskoka.

All of Tondern Island, where the cottage is located, was purchased for $101 from the Crown in 1868 by Paul Dawe.

In 1873, the whole 338-acre property was sold to Edward Prowse for $1,560. In 1885, Prowse divided up some of the property and sold it in lots. A number of summer homes were built and some of those who purchased property were from the Pittsburgh area in Pennsylvania. Some members of the Hilliard family (Elsie's grandparents) first visited Beaumaris in 1902, staying with the Mellon family on Squirrel Island. The senior Hilliards purchased their summer home on Tondern Island in 1903 and named it for their children, Henry (Raymond), Mary, Thomas and Laura Hilliard, "Ra Ma To La." In the summer of 1904, the Hilliard family first stayed at Ramatola and the cottage has been the summer home for Hilliard descendants since that time.

This magnificent century home is now enjoyed by granddaughter Elsie Hillman, her husband Henry and their family.

The Hillmans have a special ritual; at the end of each day the family gathers on the front verandah to enjoy the sunset and to discuss the day's events. It's a happy time for all.

I hope these delightful people will be here in Muskoka for many years to come.

Tuesday August 20

Most of us know how important it is to exercise, but these thoughts from Joseph Haggerty, M.D., sports medicine specialist, really hit me.

"If we could offer a pill to lengthen people's lives, decrease tension, improve work productivity and give them a method to get rid of destructive habits such as smoking, and if that pill were without harmful side effects and free, I'll bet everyone would take it in an instant. The truth is that the pill is already available—it is exercise!"

Doctors agree that the most effective exercises for general conditioning are walking, swimming and cycling. Done on a regular basis, these exercises become that "magic pill."

Wednesday August 21

The clock of life is wound but once,
And no man has the power
To tell just when the hands will stop
On what day—or what hour.
Now is the only time you have
So live it with a will.
Don't wait until tomorrow
The hands may then be still.

Anonymous

Thursday August 22

Eleanor and I enjoy a friendship that has endured for decades. We have been there for each other in good times and in bad, in times of joy and times of sorrow. We share a common love of family, friends and life. Many have written their thoughts on life and today I offer you just a few of those I find special.

Life is ours to be spent, not to be saved.

D. H. Lawrence

Life is like playing a violin in public and learning the instrument as one goes along.

Samuel Butler

Life is what happens to us while we are making other plans.

Thomas la Mance

There is no cure for birth and death, save to enjoy the interval.

George Santayana

The Indian Summer of life should always be a little sunny and a little sad, like the season, and infinite in wealth and depth of tone—but never hustled.

Henry Adams

Friday August 23

People cannot learn by having information pressed into their brains. Knowledge has to be sucked in, not pushed in. First, one must create a state of mind that craves knowledge, interest and wonder. You can teach only by creating an urge to know.

Victor Weisskopf

Saturday August 24

As wonderful as it has been to spend time with Eleanor, I am happy to be back at home this evening. I find that there is almost nothing that can take the place of your own bed at night, your own china tea cup and a walk in a garden that you have helped create.

Other places may be more beautiful, have greener grass or more spectacular gardens—but nothing can replace the home or room of your own.

Oliver Wendell Holmes wrote:

"What we love is home. Home is where our feet may leave but not our hearts."

Sunday August 25

Gladness of the heart is the life of man, and the joyfulness of a man prolongeth his days.

Ecclesiasticus 33:22

Monday August 26

Tonight as Marg and I went walking there was a definite chill in the air. As well, the sun has been sinking a little earlier each night. These signals that summer is fading and that autumn will soon arrive, I greet with mixed emotions. Autumn is a splendid time of year. Who doesn't love the magnificent colours, the bountiful harvests? But I, for one, will greatly miss the warm, lazy days of summer.

"From early freshness through the heat of noon, to lingering twilight—summer goes too soon."

Author unknown

Tuesday August 27

A rock pile ceases to be a rock pile the moment a single man contemplates it, bearing within him the image of a cathedral.

Antoine de Saint-Exupéry

Wednesday August 28

Not for one single day
Can I discern my way,
But this I surely know—
Who gives the day
Will show the way,
    So I securely go.

John Oxenham

Thursday August 29

A man would do well to carry a pencil in his pocket and write down the thoughts of the moment. Those that come unsought are commonly the most valuable and should be secured because they seldom return.

Francis Bacon

Friday August 30

Today begins the last of the summer long weekends.

Our neighbourhood once again rings with the joyous shouts of children who have come home from family vacations or camp, ready to return to school on Tuesday.

A number of my friends now reside in adult-only residences or in older neighbourhoods where there are few, if any, children.

How I would miss the happy young voices and childish enthusiasms. I am so grateful to live in a community where there are families of all ages.

Saturday August 31

The only good luck that many great men ever had was being born with the ability and determination to overcome bad luck.

Channing Pollack

September

Sunday September 1

Father, thank you for your spirit,
Fill us with his love and power;
Change us into Christ's own image
Day by day and hour by hour.

Monday September 2

These lines from Helen Keller, for me, represent very clearly the reason that Labour Day is a day for celebration.

"My share of the work of the world may be limited, but the fact that it is work makes it precious. Darwin could work only half an hour at a time; yet in many diligent half-hours he laid anew the foundation of philosophy.

Green, the historian, tells us that the world is moved, not only by the mighty shoves of the heroes, but also by the aggregate of the tiny pushes of each hard worker."

Tuesday September 3

This is the first morning of school for the children in our area. Marg and I enjoyed our tea on the front porch as we watched the youngsters go by in their "first-day finest."

What do we hope that the students will learn? In a fast-paced and ever-changing world, children need so much more than basic skills of reading, writing and arithmetic. Along with the intellectual training, young people need the experience of getting along with others from many backgrounds and cultures. They need to see the values of hard work, persistence and optimism.

Students need to learn about taking risks. The first risk is in meeting unfamiliar faces and learning to forge relationships with new teachers, other students and support staff members.

Further risk comes in small details: perseverance on a homework assignment, making individual choices in the face of peer pressure, building a set of values true to trust and responsibility and doing the right thing even when it gets very tough.

Our young people will need all of this preparation if they are to make their way confidently into the future.

I hope that today will be the first day of experiences that will lead them to reach out to the challenges of the future with hope and commitment to excellence.

AT THE FALL FAIR

Wednesday September 4

One looks back with appreciation to the brilliant teachers, but with gratitude to those who touched our human feelings. The curriculum is so much necessary raw material, but warmth is a vital element for the growing plant and for the soul of a child.

Carl Jung

Thursday September 5

When the morning returns, call us up with morning faces and with morning hearts eager to labour, happy if happiness be our portion and if the day be marked for sorrow, strong to endure.

Robert Louis Stevenson

Friday September 6

My son-in-law John amused me with this story today.

A minister asked several members of his congregation what they would like friends and family to say at their funeral.

"I would like them to say that I was a fine surgeon and a wonderful family man," said one.

"I would like to hear that by being a teacher, I made a difference in the lives of my students," said another.

"Those are very nice thoughts," said the third, "but I'd like to hear them say, 'O look, he's moving!'"

Saturday September 7

And may I tread my homeward mile—
A windy avenue's dark aisle—
Foretasting in the beechen gloom
A pleasant and a friendly room;

Where I shall find (the gods are good)
A fire of cleanly apple-wood;
And muffins—once again—for tea,
And somebody to welcome me.

Patrick R. Chalmers

Sunday September 8

God is our refuge and strength, a very present help in trouble.

Therefore will not we fear, though the earth be removed, and though the mountains be carried into the midst of the sea.

Psalm 46:1–2

Monday September 9

Didn't you find it true that just when you think tomorrow will never come, it's yesterday?

Tuesday September 10

I thought you might be interested to know that on this date in 1913, the first coast-to-coast highway in the United States was proclaimed open. It was named the Lincoln Highway.

At the time, many of the roads were dirt ones, easily washed away, and trips that might be a few short hours today could take many days.

It is difficult to imagine that the myriad interstate thruways and paved highways that crisscross that vast country, have come into being since that momentous opening so long ago.

For someone of my age, it seems miraculous.

Wednesday September 11

Potatoes have always been one of my favourite foods. In times when George's salary was small, potatoes, served in a multitude of ways, became a staple portion of many of our meals. Inexpensive and filling, they are such a versatile food that they may be enjoyed in many shapes and forms. Potato rösti, a Swiss potato dish, is a particular favourite of mine.

Potato Rösti

4 large potatoes, peeled, cooked and cooled
to room temperature
1 medium onion finely chopped
1/2 tsp. each salt, nutmeg

Black pepper to taste
4 tbsp. melted butter

Grate potatoes by hand into a medium bowl. Mix in onion, salt, nutmeg and pepper.

Heat two tablespoons butter in an 8-inch nonstick frying pan over medium heat. Add potato mixture and flatten to cover the bottom of the pan. Cook 10 minutes until the bottom surface is well browned. Shake the pan frequently to prevent sticking.

Slide the potato pancake on a large plate. Cover with another plate and flip carefully. Add remaining butter to the pan, slide pancake back into the pan, browned side up. Cook 8 to 10 minutes, shaking pan to prevent sticking.

Slide onto a serving platter. Cut into wedges. Makes 4 servings.

Thursday September 12

Money and time are the hardest burdens of life, and the unhappiest of all mortals are those who have more of either than they know how to use.

Author unknown

Friday September 13

This is one of those infrequent times when the thirteenth day of the month falls on a Friday, and our thoughts turn to the phenomenon of luck. Since many people consider this day to be an unlucky one, I thought I would offer some very wise thoughts on luck.

> The man who depends on luck will soon have nothing else to depend on.
> A little more drive, a little more pluck, a little more work—that's luck.
> Luck is the corner where preparation meets opportunity.
> People with luck usually turn out to have manufactured most of it themselves.
> Good luck will often follow the man who doesn't include it in his plan.

Saturday September 14

At this time of year, our family gets a great deal of pleasure from the fall fair. There is always something for each of us to enjoy. The children love to see the animals while many of the adults head straight to the displays of the farm produce. Marg, Julia, Mary and I like to see the many arts and crafts presentations.

What we all enjoy most is the opportunity to taste some of the delicious fruits and vegetables that are so plentiful at this time of year. At noon, we took advantage of the beautiful weather to eat our picnic lunch at the outdoor tables provided.

The horse show took our attention for the afternoon and then it was on to the heated barn, where a luscious turkey dinner was served by the dedicated ladies of the local church.

The tables were laden with platters of turkey, bowls of dressing and mashed potatoes, beans, carrots, corn and, for dessert, hot apple or peach pie with cream.

One of the most enjoyable aspects of the supper was that we had a chance to meet people who were visitors from other towns or areas of our province. The good food and fine fellowship made for a wonderful ending to a very enjoyable day.

"I close my eyes at night and say,
Thank you, God, for a lovely day."

Sunday September 15

Sing to the Lord of harvest, sing songs of love
and praise
With joyful hearts and voices, your hallelu-
jahs raise.
By him the rolling seasons in fruitful order
move;

Sing to the Lord of harvest, a joyful song of
   love.

John Samuel Monsell

Monday September 16

Teachers come in assorted sizes, weights and colours. They have various interests, hobbies, religions, and beliefs, but they share one creed: to help each child to reach the highest possible degree of personal development.

Jane C. Butler

Tuesday September 17

For many people in the business world, the responsibilities of their job may seem at times to be overwhelming. It is a clever man who is able to delegate authority and allow others to share the load.

Theodore Roosevelt made this wise observation:

"The best executive is one who has sense enough to pick good men to do what he wants done and self-restraint enough to keep from meddling with them while they do it."

Wednesday September 18

Marg and I like to do volunteer work at our local school and nearby nursing home. We both feel that we receive as much as we give in the hours spent with the children and the elderly patients who have become our friends.

We are very fortunate in our country to have volunteers who fill many positions of importance in all areas of our communities.

There are mothers who help supervise school trips. There are men and women who organize fundraisers for numerous charitable organizations. High-school scholars act as peer coaches for other less able students. Hospital "candy stripers" bring smiles and juice to patients when a nurse may be too busy. Volunteers fill a need where the costs would be prohibitive if they were to be paid for their time, even at a minimum wage.

A Statistics Canada survey showed that more than 3 million persons work over 400 million hours of volunteer unpaid service. The cost of these hours, were they paid, would have to come directly from the taxpayers.

If you have even a few hours to spare, volunteering can be a most rewarding addition to your day.

In the words of Charles Dudley Warner:

"It is one of the beautiful compensations of this life that no one can sincerely try to help another without helping himself."

Thursday September 19

Often we fret over what might have been. As we get older, it is sometimes frustrating to know that some of our dreams will never be realized.

My dear friend Lila has a wonderful attitude and I appreciate her thoughts.

"You know, Edna, when I was younger, I thought that I would be a nurse. But when my mother became ill and passed away at an early age, I felt that my responsibility was to my younger brothers and sister. I stayed at home and cared for my younger siblings.

"Later, after I married and had children, I was so involved in raising my family that I gave up any thought I had of becoming a nurse.

"Now, as I look back, I really have no regrets. I helped my father when he needed me most, I was the best wife and mother that I knew how to be and I have wonderful children and grandchildren who make me proud. Perhaps I would have been a good nurse, but I think that I have fulfilled a role that was perfect for me. I have loved the life I have lived and would never wish for anything to be different."

Lila is a remarkable lady!

Friday September 20

Tickle it with a hoe and it will laugh into a harvest.

English proverb

Saturday September 21

Although the autumnal equinox sometimes plays games with the calendar, and autumn sneaks in a day late or a day early, this is the usual day for welcoming the new season.

Although I have used these lines before, this poem remains one of my favourites for the season.

Indian Summer

Along the line of smoky hills
The crimson forest stands,
And all the day the blue jay calls
Throughout the autumn lands.

Now by the brook the maple leans
With all his glory spread,
And all the sumacs on the hills
Have turned to green and red.

Now by the great marshes wrapt in mist,
Or past some river's mouth,
Throughout the long, still autumn day
Wild birds are flying south.

Wilfred Campbell

Sunday September 22

You have crowned the year with your bounty,
and your paths overflow with a rich harvest;
the untilled meadows overflow with it, and
rejoicing clothes the hills.

Adapted from Psalm 65:12–14

Monday September 23

Listening is as important as talking. If you are
a good listener, people often compliment
you for being a good conversationalist.

Tuesday September 24

Christian faith is a grand cathedral with divinely pictured windows. Standing without, you can see no glory, nor can imagine any, but standing within every ray of light reveals a harmony of unspeakable splendours.

Nathaniel Hawthorne

Wednesday September 25

I enjoyed this anecdote from my daughter Mary.

"At church on a Sunday morning, the minister, knowing that hunting season had ended, asked who had bagged a deer.

When no one responded, the minister said, 'You know many of you missed church last week because you were hunting. Our entire congregation prayed for your deer.'

One of the hunters replied, 'Well it must have worked, they are all safe.'"

Thursday September 26

There is no reason to dread the passage of time. Age should be the rich happy fulfillment of life—the shining consummation of all that has gone before.

The opportunities for older people are greater

now than at any other time in our history, and it is up to us to make use of these opportunities.

From Lin Yutang:

"There is nothing more beautiful in this world than a healthy, wise old man."

Friday September 27

Bruce and Marshall continue to enjoy the occasional golf game even though the weather has cooled considerably.

The last time they played, one of Marshall's colleagues, a new golfer, was playing in their foursome. Time after time, Roger would put his brand new golf balls into the pond, or out of bounds in a field or into the woods—where they were never seen again.

Finally, Bruce suggested that Roger might be wise to use an old ball for his more difficult shots.

"An old ball?" Roger laughed, "Do I look like I have ever had an old ball?"

Saturday September 28

Nothing great was ever achieved without enthusiasm.

Ralph Waldo Emerson

Sunday September 29

This morning we celebrated Harvest Festival in our church. I very much enjoyed this hymn for today.

> We plough the fields and scatter
> The good seed on the land,
> But it is fed and watered
> By God's almighty hand;
> He sends the snow in winter
> The warmth to swell the grain,
> The breezes and sunshine,
> And soft refreshing rain.
> All good gifts around us
> Are sent from heaven above,
> Then thank the Lord, O thank the Lord.
> For all His love.

Jane Montgomery Campbell

Monday September 30

As September ends, autumn is truly upon us. Looking out the window, I see the most visible changes. Our maple tree is a brilliant shade of red. This tree, for whatever reason, always seems to take on a dazzling colour earlier than the rest of the trees in our yard. Each year this old maple stands out like a first-place ribbon on a child's chest.

While I love to see the magnificent colours, I

feel a twinge of sadness knowing that it won't be long before the leaves will be gone. I guess for now it is best to enjoy the beauty that will shortly disappear.

October

Tuesday October 1

The leaves of autumn whisper,
They flip and dip along
In happy lilting rhythm,
To autumn's old sweet song.

It seems they rollick, frolic,
Like children at their play;
See how autumnal breezes
Send many on their way.

The red, the gold, the copper,
The scattered shades of brown;
I gather up a handful
All while they're drifting down.

Give me the gladsome autumn,
Show me the leaves at play,
The beauty of October,
In vibrant colour display.

Georgia B. Adams

Wednesday October 2

I received a letter today from a dear friend who is living in Alberta. I wonder how many of you know how this western province was named. I found this information in a history book a number of years ago and think it is very interesting.

The province of Alberta was named by the Marquis of Lorne, (who was our governor general from 1878–1883), for his wife H. R. H. Princess Louise Caroline Alberta. After a visit to the West, he wrote:

> "In token of the love which thou hast shown
> For this wide land of freedom, I have named
> A province vast, and for its beauty famed,
> By thy dear name to be hereafter known."

Thursday October 3

I attended a local art exhibit recently and I was reminded of my great-grandson, who some years ago was also visiting an art show. Geoffrey and his mother were standing in front of one of the more abstract paintings.

"What is that supposed to be?"

His mother, June, explained, "It is supposed to be a horse and rider in a field."

"Well then," asked Geoffrey, "why isn't it?"

That boy is an art critic after my own heart.

Friday October 4

October is a spectacular month, our autumn's last blaze of glory.

Marg and I went for a walk along the Bruce Trail today and it was a beautiful hike. We didn't go a long distance as I find walking on an uneven surface is becoming more difficult, but it was a spectacularly beautiful stroll.

The air was crisp, but the sun warmed us as we made our way along the trail. The fallen leaves crackled under our feet and the smell of the damp earth brought back memories of autumns past. I was reminded of these few lines from Helen Hunt Jackson.

O sun and skies and clouds of June,
And flowers of June together,
Ye cannot rival for one hour,
October's bright blue weather.

Saturday October 5

If you don't have the time to do something right, when will you have the time to do it over?

Sunday October 6

Bless, O Lord, this food to our use,
and consecrate us to Thy service, and make

us ever mindful of the needs of others,
through Jesus Christ our Lord.

An Ancient Blessing

Monday October 7

No man or woman can really be strong, gentle, pure and good without the world being better for it, without someone being helped and comforted by the very existence of that goodness.

Phillips Brooks

Tuesday October 8

My husband, George, and I very rarely argued. This was due in part, I think, to George's particularly calm and peaceful nature, and also to several rules that we had for any argument.

Rule number one: Pick the right time to discuss things. Avoid times when you are tired or hungry; choose a good time between you.

Rule number two: Listen to the other person's feelings without interrupting or making judgments.

Rule number three: Call a time-out if either is really not listening to the other. It could be that one person is too upset to listen at that time.

Rule number four (our most important rule): Never let the sun set on your anger.

Wednesday October 9

How cherished the home where the family is valued and everyone knows he belongs.

Thursday October 10

My friend Jake Frampton gave me this list to explain the difference between Canadians and Americans.

Signs that you are Canadian:

1. You stand in "line-ups" at the movies, not lines.
2. You eat a chocolate bar, not a candy bar.
3. You understand the phrase, "Could you please pass me a serviette, I spilled my poutine."
4. You buy milk in bags.
5. You know what a "Robertson" screw driver is.
6. You know that a pike is a fish and not some kind of highway.
7. You know that Mounties don't always wear jodhpurs and red jackets.
8. You get excited when any American show mentions Canada.
9. You can eat more than one maple sugar candy without feeling nauseated.
10. You have Canadian Tire money in your wallet.
11. You know that Toronto is not a province.

GETTING READY FOR WINTER

12. You watch *Coach's Corner* and actually like Don Cherry.
13. You drive on a highway, not a freeway.
14. You sit on a couch, not a sofa.
15. You "correct" the spelling in any books that were written in the USA by adding the missing "u" in color, labor and honor.

Friday October 11

During the harvest month, I often think back to our days in a rural parish on Canada's east coast. For the most part, farmers and their families would get together to become one large crew, moving from farm to farm to harvest the ripe crops.

Harvest dinners, provided by the women of the family, were a part of each working day. Usually the women would cook at home in their own kitchen, preparing some part of the noon meal. They would then carry the hot dishes to the cloth-covered tables set out where the crop-picking was taking place.

The women became quite clever at keeping the dishes hot during the long trips from their farm kitchens. Some used a "straw cooker"— loose straw packed in a wooden box with the covered dish set in a hollow in the straw, covered with more straw and a lid for the box screwed on tightly. Others used something called a "freestone." Soapstones were heated on a kitchen stove and then placed in a small metal tub. Pots of food set on the stones stayed hot for hours. These meals were marvels of organization and a tribute to the old saying, "Many hands make light work."

Saturday October 12

I believe the future is only the past again, entered through another gate.

Arthur Wing Pinero

Sunday October 13

I enjoyed singing an old favourite hymn this morning at church. With so much to be thankful for, I sang with an especially joyful heart on this day.

Now thank we all our God,
With heart and hands and voices,
Who wondrous things hath done,
In whom his world rejoices;
Who from his mother's arms
Hath blessed us on our way
With countless gifts of love,
And still is ours today.

Rev. Martin Rinkart

Monday October 14

Thanksgiving is a day we McCanns really enjoy. Along with Christmas, it is a day when the largest number of our family members get together. It is a happy time of delicious meals, fellowship and hour after hour of "Remember the time...?"

I can think of nothing that I enjoy more than the company of my children, grandchildren and great-grandchildren. I have so much to be thankful for and I hope that you, too, have many reasons to celebrate this special day.

In the words of Charles L. Swindoll:

"Thanksgiving is a time of quiet reflection... an annual reminder that God has, again, been ever so faithful."

Tuesday October 15

If I had a formula for by-passing trouble, I would not pass it around. Trouble creates a capacity to handle it. I don't say embrace trouble; that's as bad as treating it as an enemy. But I do say meet it as a friend, for you'll see a lot of it and had better be on speaking terms with it.

Oliver Wendell Holmes, Jr.

Wednesday October 16

When you say that you've troubles as great as
   my own,
I'm forced to admit that it's true,
But consider the fact that mine happen to me
While yours merely happen to you.

Thursday October 17

Ideals are like stars. You will not succeed in touching them with your hands, but like the seafaring man on the ocean desert of waters, you choose them as your guides, and following them, reach your destiny.

Carl Schurz

Friday October 18

This is a wonderful time of the year for decorating around the home. Pumpkins, gourds, flowers and coloured leaves can combine to make simple, but attractive, decorations for both inside and outside your home.

A pumpkin makes a very handsome vase for fall flowers. Cut the top off the pumpkin and scoop out the seeds and flesh. Put a jar of water inside the pumpkin and then arrange a bouquet of brightly coloured chrysanthemums with some greenery. This bouquet looks lovely on an outside porch or deck.

Any dining-room table looks very festive with an assortment of candles in gourd candle-holders. Gourds in assorted sizes and colours may be found at markets everywhere. Cut a slice off the bottom in order to make the gourd stable and then carve a hole in the top. Insert tapers of many colours and you have a very attractive centrepiece for a special dinner.

Grapevine wreaths with coloured leaves, bowls of red and green polished apples, or straw wreaths with pressed and waxed leaves are just a few ways to take advantage of October's bounty when decorating your home.

Saturday October 19

The hills of October gleam in the sun,
Flashing from dawn till the good day is done,
Brown they gleam in the shocks of corn,
Heavy with frost in the early morn.

Golden they gleam with the golden rod,
Silvery white with milkweed pod.
Crimson and yellow in maple and gum,
They gleam a cry of, "Come! Come! Come!"

Gleaming apples in yellow and reds,
Rich brown nuts in brown leaf beds.
Gleaming streams by gay asters pass,
And smile at the crests of the soft brown
    grass.

A gleaming leaf falls; a gleaming shower,
Falling like rain, started that hour.
Oh, the hills of October gleam in the sun,
Flashing the cry that summer is done.

Barton Rees Pogue

Sunday October 20

We all, with open face beholding as in a glass the glory of the Lord, are changed into the same image from glory to glory, even as by the Spirit of the Lord.

II Corinthians 3:18

Monday October 21

Write it on the heart that every day is the best day in the year.

Ralph Waldo Emerson

Tuesday October 22

I was remembering today a very dear friend who passed away two years ago. Bernard "Bernie" McKinnon was a professor at St. Lawrence University in Canton, New York. Born in Dartmouth, Nova Scotia, he was a member of the St. Lawrence men's hockey team that played in the NCAA tournament in 1954–55 and was team captain in 1956–57.

After two years in the U.S. army and a stint in the business world, he returned to St. Lawrence in the athletic department. He was a professor of sport and leisure studies and over the next 30 years, he coached many teams in a number of sports. He was a champion of women's athletics and was the first coach of the women's soccer team and the women's ice hockey team when these sports were added to St. Lawrence. Over the years, Bernie was a "College Coach of the Year," a winner of the Joe Burke award for outstanding contributions to women's hockey and, just two weeks before his death, was inducted into the Athletic Hall of Fame for St. Lawrence University.

Bernie and his wife, Lennelle ("Lennie"), were a wonderful inspiration for the women and men that Bennie coached. Neither Bernie nor Lennie was particularly wrapped up in winning or losing. Bernie was sincerely interested in the excellent play of his teams, and Lennie was always the team's number-one fan. No one was more vociferous in their support than Lennie!

Bernie was a people-magnet who loved to make new friends, and would remember them always. It seemed that no matter what one wanted to do, Bernie knew just the right person to talk to and would not rest until he had touched base with that person. Just hours before he passed away, Bernie was recruiting a son of one of his nurses for the St. Lawrence hockey team.

Bernie and Lennie were often surrogate parents for all of the team members and his influence is sorely missed. My thoughts go to Lennie today and I know that around the United States and Canada, a number of young men and women who were lucky enough to be coached by this kind and caring man will pause and remember with thanks a man who instilled in them a love of sport for sport's sake and a commitment to excellence, no matter what the score.

Wednesday October 23

A well-balanced life is one which fails to give you what you ask for about as often as it fails to give you what you deserve.

F. Walsh

Thursday October 24

Marg and I enjoyed watching the football game at the high school today. My great-grandson Justin and his teammates won a very hard-fought battle with their cross-town rivals. I couldn't help but think how proud George would have been.

For several years, George was a coach at the high school in our parish. He put a lot of stock in effort and attitude. Any young man who failed to give his all in practice often found himself sitting on the bench during the game. The boys soon realized that hard work and positive attitude earned just as much success as athletic brilliance.

These young men learned a lesson in life as well as in football.

Friday October 25

The significance of a man is not in what he attains, but rather in what he longs to attain.

Saturday October 26

I thank the unknown author for these lines on friendship.

Friendship is a golden chain,
The links are friends so dear,
And like a rare and precious jewel,
It's treasured more each year...
It's clasped together firmly
With a love that's deep and true,
And it's rich with happy memories
And fond recollections too...
Time can't destroy its beauty
For as long as a memory lives,
Years can't erase the pleasure
That the joy of friendship gives...
For friendship is a precious gift,
That can't be bought or sold,
But to have an understanding friend
Is worth far more than gold...

And the golden chain of friendship
Is a strong and blessed tie
Binding kindred hearts together
As the years go passing by.

Sunday October 27

Honour the Lord with thy substance, and with the first fruits of all thine increase: So shall thy barns be filled with plenty, and thy presses shall burst out with new wine.

Proverbs 3:9–10

Monday October 28

October is the month for painted leaves—as fruits and leaves and the day itself acquire a bright tint just before they fall, so the year nears its setting. October is its sunset sky; November the later twilight.

Henry David Thoreau

Tuesday October 29

Many people have written about Abraham Lincoln's wisdom and simplicity, but none I think, more eloquently than Ralph Waldo Emerson.

"His heart was as great as the world, but there was no room in it to hold a memory of wrong."

Wednesday October 30

Bruce spent several hours this evening carving our pumpkin with Bethany and Michael. I have to say that Bruce is one of the most patient people I know. Michael is a young lad who is "full of beans" and not able to sit still for any length of time, but when he is with his "Grampa," he seems much more able to focus his attention on whatever task the two of them are tackling. Perhaps it's Bruce's calm demeanour, or the tone of his voice that Michael finds soothing, but whatever it is, Michael is as good as gold when he and "Gramps" are together.

Michael, Beth and Bruce did a wonderful job on our jack-o-lantern and it will be proudly displayed on our front porch tomorrow.

Thursday October 31

Oh, just to span the years between
And go back home for Halloween!
The low brown house, the willow tree,
The welcome that there used to be!
To taffy pulls and pleasures gay...
Quaint joys that vanished yesterday!
Oh, just to span the years between
And go back home for Halloween!

Author unknown

November

Friday November 1
All Saints Day

We thank Thee, O God, for the saints of all ages; for those who, in times of darkness, kept the lamp of faith burning; for the great souls who saw visions of larger truth and dared to declare it; for the multitude of quiet and glorious souls whose presence has purified and sanctified the world; and for those known and loved by us who have passed from this earthly fellowship into the fuller light of life with Thee. Amen.

Saturday November 2

The wild November comes at last
Beneath a veil of rain;
The night wind blows its folds aside,
Her face is full of pain.
The latest of her race, she takes
The autumn's vacant throne;
She has but one short moon to live,
And she must live alone.

R. H. Stoddard

Sunday November 3

From the rising of the sun unto the going down of the same the Lord's name is to be praised!

The Lord is high above all nations, and His glory above the heavens.

Psalm 113:3–4

Monday November 4

I have picked up a miserable flu bug from somewhere and because I was feeling so wretched, I needed to see our family doctor. As I dragged my aching body out to the car and then into the doctor's office, I had a fond thought for the breed of doctor that has all but vanished—the physician who makes house calls.

I grew up in a era when all doctors made house calls. We knew that when we sent for the doctor, he would come if it were at all possible. The weather, personal convenience or hour of the day was of no consideration.

For years, the family doctor enjoyed an exalted position in the community because of his close association with his patients, his participation in their joys and griefs and their confidence in his skills. Of course the health-care system has expanded and changed so much over the years that house calls, unless one lives in a remote rural area, are unheard of.

I have every confidence in our family physician, a skilled professional, but I confess that I would have enjoyed a house call today. I don't like to suffer in silence and, somehow, moaning in the waiting room seemed less than dignified.

Tuesday November 5

In today's world, many families have members who are scattered to the far corners of the earth. I believe that those of us who are missing our loved ones may find comfort in these words of Oliver Wendell Holmes.

> And where we love is home,
> Home that our feet may leave, but not our hearts,
> The chain may lengthen, but it never parts.

Wednesday November 6

We have a course offered for families at our local library called "Conversation—*not* a lost art." Our librarian remarked that she was surprised by the number of people who signed up, but in thinking about it, I can understand why some families feel the need to practise conversational skills.

We have a multitude of conversation substitutes in our homes today: computers, televisions, radios, Walkmans and more. Often, as well, both parents are working and the opportunities for meaningful conversation are few.

There is nothing more important in family life than communication with one another. If this course can provide help in that vital area of our lives it will be beneficial—not just now, but for the years to come.

Thursday November 7

The best thing about the future is that it comes only one day at a time.

Friday November 8

I am only just now starting to feel a little better after my bout with the flu. It's amazing how debilitating an influenza bug can be—I even believed that my eyelashes were aching. The only nice thing about spending a number of days in bed is that when you are finally able to get up and about, the world around you looks especially beautiful, no matter how dreary the weather.

In the words of George Bernard Shaw:

"I enjoy convalescence. It is the part that makes illness worthwhile."

Saturday November 9

Getting older is like being swept out to sea. At one point you want to get to the horizon to see what's there. Then you arrive and you suddenly realize there's no way back.

Timothy Findley

Sunday November 10

Almighty God, from whom all thoughts of truth and peace proceed: Kindle we pray thee, in the hearts of all men the true love of peace, and guide with thy pure and peaceful wisdom those who take counsel for the nations of the earth; that in tranquility thy kingdom may go forward, till the earth is filled with the knowledge of thy love; through Jesus Christ our Lord. Amen.

"A prayer for peace"
from The Book of Common Prayer

Monday November 11
Remembrance Day

This is the day when we pause to remember all those who gave their lives in the two world wars. Across our country memorial wreaths will be laid at cenotaphs, and those brave men and women (fewer in number each year) who fought for the rights and freedoms that we enjoy today will remember the friends and comrades who never returned.

"In peace, sons bury their fathers; in war, fathers bury their sons."

Herodotus

Tuesday November 12

An adventure is only an inconvenience rightly considered. An inconvenience is only an adventure wrongly considered.

G. K. Chesterton

I thought of these words today as my son-in-law John recounted the story of his airline flight to New York City. Because of bad weather, the flight was diverted to Boston. In Boston, passengers were offered a night's stay in a hotel and an early-morning flight to New York the next day. Unlike many of his fellow travellers, who were quite put out by the delay, John took advantage of his evening in Boston to enjoy a meal at a seafood restaurant, a swim in the hotel pool and a comfortable evening in his room. He enjoyed his "adventure" very much.

Wednesday November 13

Several years ago, a made-for-TV movie called *Summer's End* was being filmed in Muskoka. The star of the film was James Earl Jones, an actor who is famous for the depth and power of his extraordinary voice.

Eleanor and I spent several days watching the production and were in awe of Mr. Jones, never more so than when he had a long monologue walking off the dock at the marina. The intensity and authority of his voice gave us both shivers!

We were very interested to learn that, from the age of nine until his mid teens, Jones stuttered so badly that he had to communicate with teachers and fellow students by writing notes.

He began to overcome his disability when his high school English teacher encouraged him to recite his own poetry in class. Quite surprisingly, he found that he was able to do so fluently.

Even now Jones explains, "Once a stutterer, always a stutterer. If I get any credit for the way I sound, I accept it in the name of those of us who are impaired."

Thurday November 14

If you have built castles in the air, your work need not be lost; that is where they should be. Now put foundations under them.

Henry David Thoreau

Friday November 15

During the month of November, I like to enjoy comfort foods. Something that fills the bill is cheesy corn bread. This is especially simple to make as I use a store-bought mix to start.

Cheesy Corn Bread

2 pkgs. (8.5 oz. each) corn muffin mix
3/4 cup buttermilk
2 eggs
1 can (11 oz.) kernel corn (drained)
1 cup shredded sharp cheddar cheese
1 large green onion finely sliced

Pre-heat the oven to 375°F. Coat a 9-inch cake pan with cooking spray. In a large bowl combine the muffin mix, buttermilk, eggs, corn and scallion pieces until the ingredients are just moistened. Spread the batter in the pan. Bake 30 minutes or until the top is golden and a toothpick inserted comes out clean. Cool in pan on rack for 10 minutes. Remove from the pan; serve warm or at room temperature. Makes 12 servings

This corn bread, served with a bowl of soup and a salad, makes a wonderful meal for a cold November night.

Saturday November 16

Nobody wants constructive criticism. It's all we can do to put up with constructive praise.

Mignon McLaughlin

Sunday November 17

Blest be the tie that binds
Our hearts in Christian love!
That fellowship of kindred minds
Is like to that above.

Rev. John Fawcett

Monday November 18

I recently read an interesting article that calculated, in percentages, how a typical lifespan of 70 years is spent. I think you'll find this estimate very interesting as well.

Sleep	23 years	32.9%
Work	16 years	22.8%
TV/Computer	8 years	11.4%
Eating	6 years	8.6%
Travel	6 years	8.6%
Leisure	4.5 years	6.5%
Illness	4 years	5.7%
Dressing	2 years	2.8%
Religion	0.5 years	0.7%

If this were your 70 years, would it reflect accurately your priorities? If not, perhaps it would be wise to make adjustments right now in the ways that your time is spent.

Our days are numbered and are meant to be used wisely. Henry Austin Dobson put it best:

"Time goes you say? Ah, no! Alas, time stays, we go."

Tuesday November 19

I am sure that if people had to choose between living where the noise of children never stopped, and where it was never heard, all the good-natured and sound people would prefer the incessant noise to the silence.

George Bernard Shaw

Wednesday November 20

Anthony Trollope expressed my feelings when he said:

"Book love, my friends, is your pass to the greatest, the purest, and the most perfect pleasure that God has prepared for his creatures. It lasts when all other pleasures fade. It will support you when all other recreations are gone. It will last you until your death. It will make your hours pleasant to you as long as you live."

Thursday November 21

Men go abroad to wonder at the height of mountains, at the huge waves of the sea, at the long courses of the rivers, at the vast compass of the ocean, at the circular motion of the stars; and they pass by themselves without wondering.

St. Augustine

Friday November 22

Confucius, the great Chinese teacher and philosopher, was born in 551 B.C. As a young man he quickly earned a fine reputation for fairness, politeness and his love of learning.

Confucius had a simple moral and political teaching: to love others, to honour one's parents, to do what is right instead of what is of advantage and to do nothing to others that you would not want done to you.

Although Confucius did not put his thoughts into writing, his wise reflections were handed down through the years by his many disciples.

I share just a few of his thoughts with you today.

The superior man is modest in his speech but exceeds in his actions.

It is not possible for one to teach others who cannot teach his own family.

If you enjoy what you do, you'll never work another day in your life.

A thousand-mile journey begins with one step.

Behave towards everyone as if receiving a great guest.

The man who removes a mountain begins by carrying away small stones.

Saturday November 23

Although it has been several years since I have driven a car myself, I always look forward to riding with my daughters, sons-in-law or my grandchildren. I have always enjoyed country drives, although I admit that riding on our major highways now has become somewhat nerve-wracking for me. Although the speed at which cars travel on our highways seems excessive, I am more frightened by what is know as "road rage" or aggressive driving.

Most of us at some time or another have experienced drivers who seem to allow their anger and frustration to influence their driving behaviour. These aggressive drivers make unsafe lane changes, run through red lights, tailgate, cut you off and generally disobey all of the rules for safe driving. These drivers put all of us who are on the highway at great risk.

Something as simple as fatigue or being late for an appointment may often trigger aggressive driving. Experts suggest that when you find yourself in a stressful driving situation, the best thing to do is to take a deep breath, try to relax and remember that it is better to "arrive alive."

At this time of year, aggressive driving may be particularly hazardous. We are just beginning a season of snow and sleet, a time when we need to slow down. Many of us forget from one year to the next that these weather conditions require extra precautions and slower speeds. Don't you become a traffic statistic! Safe driving is everyone's responsibility.

Sunday November 24

If ye keep my commandments, ye shall abide in My love.... These things I have spoken unto you, that my joy might remain in you, and that your joy might be full.

John 15:10–11

Monday November 25

Pride makes us do things well, but it is love that makes us do them to perfection.

Tuesday November 26

This evening a young neighbour dropped by to collect empty bottles for his Boy Scout troop. Seeing him in his uniform reminded me of Lord Baden-Powell, the founder of the Boy Scouts. Former readers may remember this story, but I think it is worth retelling.

When Lord Baden-Powell died in Africa, his family was offered a burial site for him in Westminster Abbey—between the graves of Britain's Unknown Soldier and David Livingstone, the eminent missionary. His family declined this great honour and chose instead a small undistinguished cemetery in Kenya. His headstone was also simple. It bore only his name, dates of birth and death and a circle with a dot in the centre. This symbol, in Boy Scout language, means "I have gone home."

Wednesday November 27

It is a good thing to be rich, and to be strong, but it is a better thing to be loved of many friends.

Euripides

Thursday November 28

This is Thanksgiving Day in the United States and I thought you might enjoy reading a letter, written to describe the Pilgrims' first Thanksgiving. It was written by Edward Winslow of Plymouth, Massachusetts, in 1621, to friends in England.

"Our harvest being gotten in, our Governor sente four men out fowling that so we might, after a more special manner, rejoyce together after we had gathered the fruit of our labours.

These four; in one day, killed as much fowl as, with a little help besides, served the company almost a week, at which time, amongst other recreations, we exercised our arms, many of the Indians amongst us.

And amongst the rest, their greatest King, Massasoit, with some ninety men, whom for three days, we entertained and feasted.

And they went out and killed five deer, which they brought to the Plantation and bestowed upon our Governor and upon the Captaine and others.

And though it be not always so plentiful as it was at this time with us, yet, by the goodness of God, we are so farr from wante that we often wish you partakers of our plentie."

Friday November 29

If we learn how to forgive ourselves, to forgive others, and to live with thanksgiving, we need not seek happiness. It will seek us.

Saturday November 30

The deeper man goes into life, the deeper is his conviction that this life is not all; it is an "unfinished symphony." A day may round out an insect's life, and a bird or beast needs no tomorrow. Not so with him who knows that he is related to God and has felt the power of an endless life.

Henry Ward Beecher

December

Sunday December 1

First Sunday in Advent

Hark the glad sound! the Saviour comes,
The Saviour promised long:
Let every heart prepare a throne,
And every voice a song.

Our glad hosannas, Prince of Peace,
Thy welcome shall proclaim;
And heaven's eternal arches ring
With Thy beloved Name. Amen

Monday December 2

There are a number of Advent traditions that have come to North America from Europe. One of our family's favourite is the Advent calendar, a German custom. These calendars may take many forms. Sometimes it is a picture of a Christmas scene with numbered windows—one is opened each day to reveal a smaller scene or perhaps a line from scripture. More popular for children are the calendars which, when a window is opened, reveal a piece of chocolate. I found a chocolate calendar for each of my great-grand-children and hope that they will enjoy their little treat as they await the big day.

Tuesday December 3

The French writer Voltaire, in his play *Candide*, referred to Canada as *"quelques arpents de neige,"* or "a few acres of snow." We who endure the Canadian winter may be tempted to agree. Those who keep track of such information have determined that snow fell in every month of the twentieth century in every province with the sole exception of Prince Edward Island, which never saw snow in July.

Is it any wonder then, that Canadians were inventors of the first train-size rotary plow, the first snow blower and the first toboggan, which was an adaptation of the sleds used by Inuit to haul heavy loads?

It was also a Canadian, J. Armand Bombardier, who changed drastically our ability to travel on snow. Born in the village of Valcourt, Quebec, Bombardier began tinkering with a motorized sled at an early age. At 15, he attached a propeller to the engine of a Model T Ford and, with this mounted on skis, travelled a little more than a mile on his first trip. This initial attempt—with an exposed propeller—was primitive and

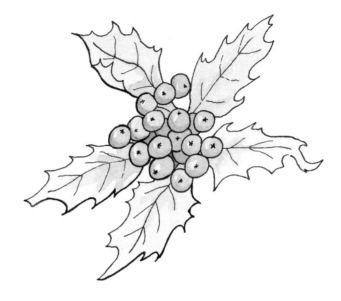

dangerous, but he continued to play with and perfect his idea. By 1937, Bombardier had patented his first multi-passenger snowmobile.

Over the years, his snowmobile evolved until, in 1958, he produced a lightweight sport vehicle which we know today as the Ski-Doo. There are now more than a half a million snowmobiles registered in Canada and many thousands of kilometres of organized trails on which to travel.

If we can't get away from winter, at least we can try to enjoy it.

Wednesday December 4

For many of us on fixed incomes, finding affordable gifts can often be quite a challenge. I like to give gifts from my kitchen, and early in December is a good time to get started on them. A homemade gourmet gift provides a special personal touch that is unavailable, even in the most exclusive shops.

Jams, jellies, cookies, cakes and candies seem to be especially welcomed gifts, as few people seem to have the time to make their own these days. Add a pretty wrapping paper and a festive bow and you'll have a handsome gift that is a pleasure to give.

Thursday December 5

This morning Marg and I filled our bird-feeder with wild bird seed and small suet balls. The feeder is a lovely wooden one that my great-grandson Mickey made for me many years ago. My son-in-law Bruce has helped me keep the feeder in good condition by frequently cleaning it and adding a coat of urethane when necessary.

We were delighted to see several blue jays and a large number of chickadees visit the feeder today. If you are able, please try to feed the birds regularly. They come to depend on us during the harsh days of our winter and I'm sure that you, like I, will rest easier each night knowing that at least some of our feathered friends have eaten well.

Friday December 6

The lives of all of us have been enriched by the many people whom we have known and loved. At this season a card or a note renews that friendship and buoys our spirits with love.

Marg and I finished our Christmas cards today and as we do each year, sealed each with a Christmas seal provided by the Canadian Lung Association. This fundraising campaign actually had its origin in 1907. At that time, Emily Bissell, a social worker, was struggling to keep open a small tuberculosis clinic in Delaware. Having heard of a special Christmas stamp that was issued in Denmark to raise money for needy children, Emily designed her own stamp that showed a holly wreath and the words "Merry Christmas." She sold the stamps in packets with the message:

Put this stamp
On every Christmas letter
Help the tuberculosis fight
And make the New Year better.

Her stamps raised more than enough money to keep her sanitarium open and with the extra funds, the National Tuberculosis Association was founded. Today, the Canadian Lung Association still uses funds raised from the Christmas Seals campaign to fight lung disease.

Saturday December 7

There is no such thing as chance; and what seems to us the merest accident springs from the deepest source of destiny.

Friedrich von Schiller

Sunday December 8

Now the God of hope fill you with all joy and peace in believing that ye may abound in hope, through the power of the Holy Ghost.

The Book of Common Prayer

Monday December 9

Old age is the snow of the earth; it must, through light and truth, give warmth to the seeds of youth below, protecting them and fulfilling their purpose.

Kahlil Gibran

Tuesday December 10

The snow had begun in the gloaming,
And busily all the night
Had been heaping field and highway
With a silence deep and white.

Every pine and fir and hemlock
Wore ermine too dear for an earl,
And the poorest twig on the elm tree
Was ridged inch deep in pearl.

James Russell Lowell

Wednesday December 11

At this time of year it's not unusual to have friends drop by to offer personal good wishes for the season. I like to have some special snacks available to serve and this next recipe for Brie and roasted garlic tastes every bit as good as it looks.

Brie and Roasted Garlic

2 whole garlic bulbs
1 – 12-oz. round of Brie cheese at room temperature
1 – 6 oz. jar roasted red peppers, drained,
or 2 to 3 whole roasted peppers cut into bite-size strips
Thin slices of toast, cut in triangles.

Pre-heat the oven to 375°F. Remove most outer

skins of the garlic bulbs, leaving the last couple of layers; do not peel down to the clove itself. Place garlic on a baking sheet and bake for about 45 minutes or until the garlic cloves are soft.

Place the Brie in the centre of a serving plate. Separate the roasted garlic cloves and place around the Brie. Arrange pepper slices and toast slices around the plate. The circular display looks like a Christmas wreath.

To eat, spread a toast slice with Brie, squeeze on roasted garlic and top with a slice of roasted pepper.

This is also a delicious appetizer to serve company at dinner.

Thursday December 12

This is such a busy time of year that spare minutes are hard to find. If you can provide just a little time, I know of some people who would enjoy sharing it with you. Nursing-home residents or those who are long-term hospital patients may be especially lonely at this time of year.

It probably takes a little more effort to find the time to make a visit at Christmas, but it is wise to remember that all of us grow older and sometime we may be the ones who yearn for companionship and love.

Friday December 13

Maybe we should do something that we think we can do well, even if we don't get praise. After all, birds sing without applause.

Saturday December 14

Bruce brought home the Christmas tree this evening, a lovely Scotch pine. We will decorate the tree today and remember the symbolic meaning of this tradition. The evergreen represents eternity, which Christ came to make real for us; the lights speak of Christ, light of the world; and the decorations declare the joy and happiness of Christ's birthday.

Sunday December 15

Heavenly Father, who chose the Virgin Mary, full of grace, to be the mother of our Lord and Saviour, now fill us with your grace, that we, in all things, may embrace your will and with her rejoice in your salvation through Jesus Christ our Lord. Amen.

The Book of Common Prayer

Monday December 16

In December ring
Every day the chimes;
Loud the gleemen sing
In the streets their merry rhymes.
Let us by the fire,
Even higher,
Sing them till the night expire.

Henry Wadsworth Longfellow

Tuesday December 17

Ninety-nine years ago today, Orville and Wilbur Wright brought to reality the century-old dream of soaring with the eagles.

Their first flight at Kitty Hawk, North Carolina, lasted but 12 seconds and went a mere 120 feet, but it signalled the beginning of a new era that has taken man to the moon and back.

William Newton Clark wrote:

"Faith is the daring of the soul to go further than it can see."

Wednesday December 18

If we can say with Seneca, "This life is only a prelude to eternity," then we need not worry so much over the fittings and furnishings of this ante-room; and more than that, it will give dignity and purpose to the fleeting days to know they are linked with the eternal things as a prelude and preparation.

Minot Judson Savage

Thursday December 19

Arrive the snow, and, driving o'er the fields
Seems nowhere to alight: the whited air
Hides hills and woods, the river, and the
    heaven,
And veils the farmhouse at garden's end.

Ralph Waldo Emerson

Friday December 20

The Jewish celebration of Hanukkah takes place around the time of the winter solstice and lasts eight days. Hanukkah celebrates religious freedom and is a special time for children—a time for song and games and gift-giving.

Lighting the candles of the "Chanukkiyah," the special candelabrum that holds the eight candles of Hanukkah, is an annual tradition in Jewish homes.

I wish for all of my Jewish friends a Happy Hanukkah and the joys of time spent with friends and family at this special time of year.

Saturday December 21

'Tis winter, yet there is no sound along the air
Of winds along their battle ground; but
  gently there
The snow is falling—all around.

Ralph Hoyt

Sunday December 22

How much I enjoy singing the carols of the Christmas season. This morning we sang one of my favourites.

"The First Noel"

The first Noel the angel did say
Was to certain poor shepherds
in fields where they lay;
In fields where they lay keeping their sheep,
On a cold winter's night that was so deep.
Noel, Noel, Noel, Noel,
Born is the King of Israel.

Monday December 23

Several youngsters came to our house this evening singing carols. Listening to their fresh young voices transported me back many years to the centre of our town where we would stand and sing to passing walkers or horse-drawn sleighs filled with passengers. If I close my eyes,

I can still see the candle lanterns that we carried and feel the crisp cold air that would turn our cheeks to roses. This is a memory that many of you, my readers, probably cherish as I do.

Tuesday December 24

This is Christmas Eve but also it is Marshall and Jamie's fourteenth wedding anniversary. Married in a small country church with only family members and close friends in attendance, it was a beautiful occasion. This evening, with Marshall, Jamie and their children Bethany and Michael, we returned to that tiny church for the Christmas Eve service.

The church was decorated, as it was then, with red and white poinsettia plants, and white tapers burning in the shiny brass chandelier. Each of us carried a white candle and, as the candles were lit one by one, the light dimmed. Finally there was only the candlelight as we sang the last hymn, "Silent Night."

As I looked at my grandchildren and great-grandchildren in the candlelight, I could feel the tears pricking my eyes.

I feel so strongly about the importance of family that it gave me tears of joy to celebrate an anniversary of two young people who are perpetuating our family tradition of happy lives together.

Wednesday December 25
Christmas Day

For unto us a child is born, unto us a son is given....

Isaiah 9:6

Thursday December 26

Christmas is such a joyous occasion in our home that we decided to do something a little special this season. Knowing how many families have to do without at this time of year, we "adopted" a local family who needed help if it was to enjoy a truly merry Christmas.

We were given a wish list from a young single mother who has two small children to provide for on a very limited income. This young woman needed such basic things as winter jackets and boots for her two boys—there was no mention of toys.

We had a wonderful time shopping for "our family." With all of our children and grandchildren involved, we were able to provide everything that had been wished for and, as well, we found many toys and special treats that we hoped would give them an especially happy day.

The Red Cross also asked that a food hamper be provided. When we mentioned to some of our friends and neighbours that we were purchasing canned goods for the hamper, everyone wanted

CHRISTMAS MORNING

to help. In just a few short days we received cases of food that should keep the family well fed for many weeks.

I really felt the spirit of Christmas as we wrapped each gift, knowing that we were making a difference in someone's life.

Giving truly is more blessed than receiving.

Friday December 27

Jake Frampton stopped in this evening and was bemoaning the fact that he "ate far too much, as usual.

"You know, Edna, I really don't think I'm over-weight, I'm simply under-tall. If I were to use the doctor's chart I believe I should be about six feet seven inches tall. Instead of going on a diet, I think I'll go home and grow six inches taller. I probably have about the same chance of that as I do of losing weight."

Saturday December 28

Joseph Haydn, when criticized for the gaiety of his church music, responded:

"I cannot help it. I give forth what is in me. When I think of the Divine Being, my heart is so full of joy that the notes fly off as from a spindle. And, as I have a cheerful heart, He will pardon me if I serve Him cheerfully."

Sunday December 29

> Glory to God in the highest,
> And on earth peace, goodwill toward men.

Monday December 30

Who can put a value on friendship? Who can measure in any kind of terms just what real friendship is worth?

True friendship doesn't require daily contact to keep alive. Have you found, as I have, that with friends of long standing, even if we've been separated for many years, we can pick up right where we left off—almost as if in mid-conversation?

As Ralph Waldo Emerson put it, "a friend may well be reckoned the masterpiece of nature."

As this year comes to an end, I remember all those people whom I call friend and I am grateful.

Tuesday December 31

Some years ago, a Jewish friend of mine shared a written greeting from her rabbi on the occasion of Rosh Hashanah, the beginning of the Jewish New Year. It read, in part:

"What has the New Year to say to us? Its simple message is: you are here! Whatever problems you may have had during the past year—illness, worry, trouble—you have survived them. You are alive, you are here and you are not alone. If you stretch out your hand, you will find love; if you reach out far enough, you will find the hand of fellowship outstretched by neighbour and friend.

May the New Year bring enough charity for you to see good in your neighbour, enough love to move you to be helpful to others and enough faith to make real the things of God."

HAPPY NEW YEAR TO YOU ALL!